CW01261867

Cara Dillon

COMING HOME

CHARCOAL PRESS

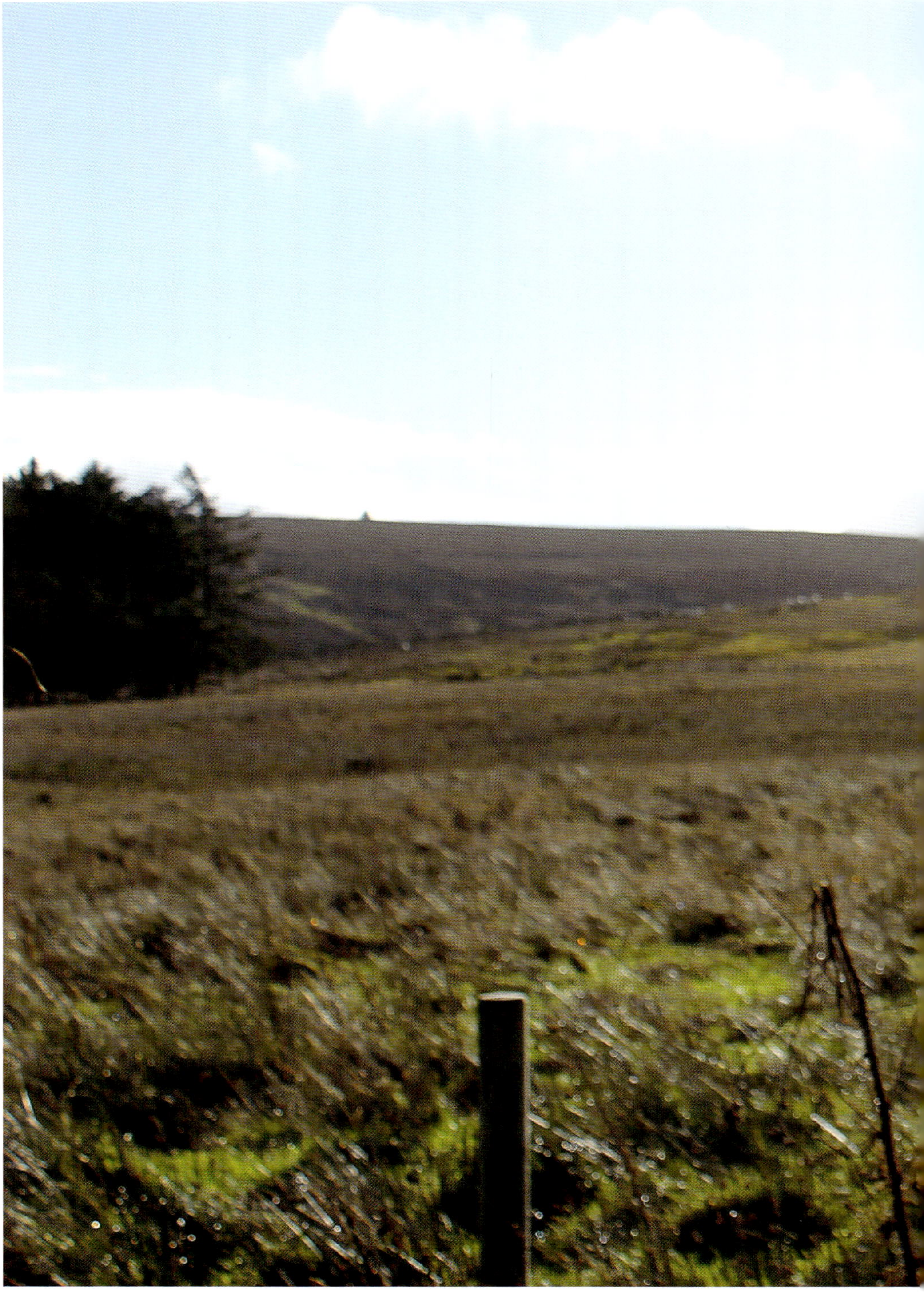

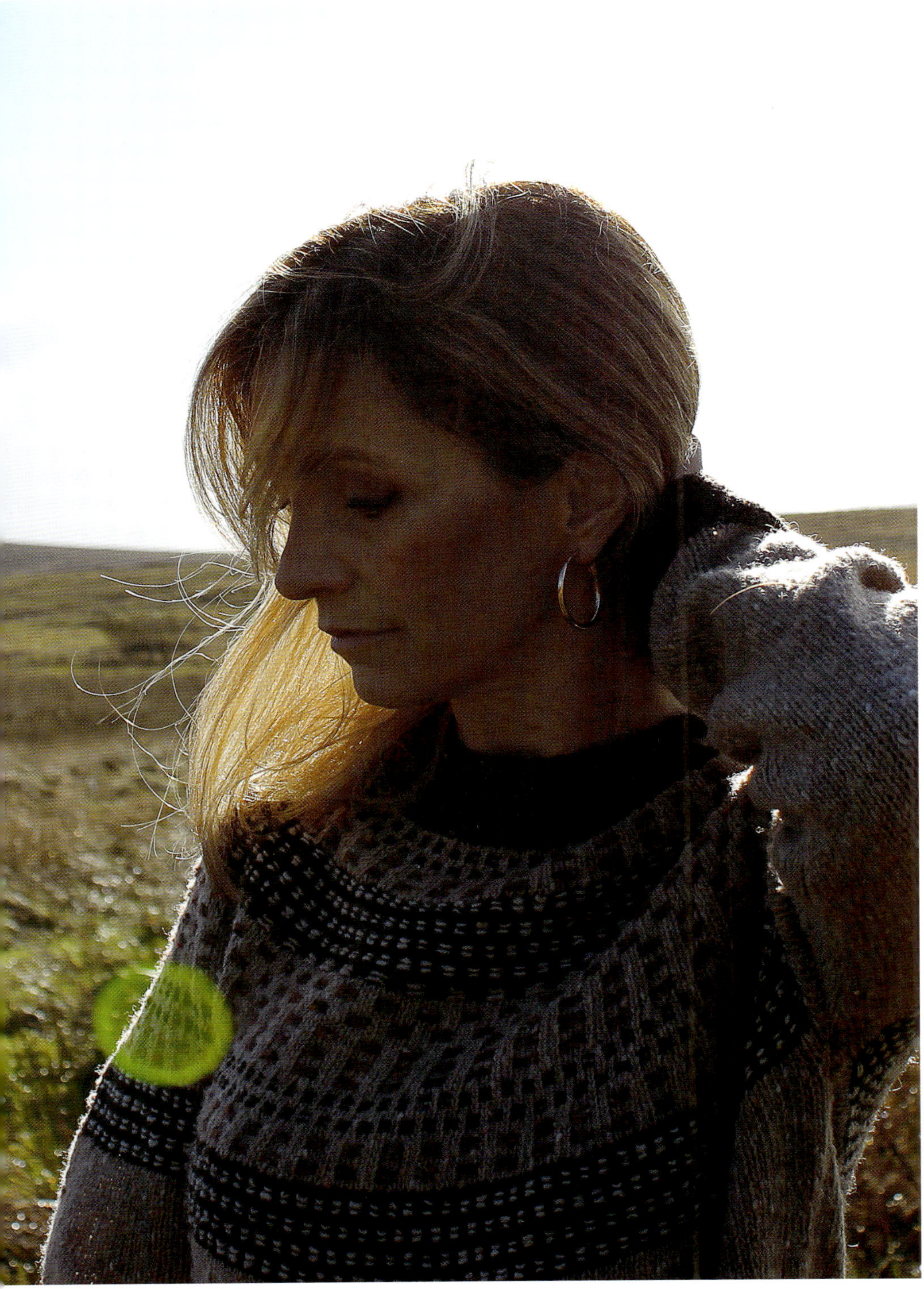

Copyright © 2023 by Cara Dillon.

First published in hardback in Great Britain in 2024

Charcoal Press, PO Box 5635, Frome, UK, BA11 9ET

The right of Cara Dillon to be identified as the author of this work has been asserted by her in accordance with the Copyright, Designs and Patents Act,1988. All rights reserved. This book is copyright material and must not be copied, reproduced, transferred, distributed, leased, licensed, or publicly performed or used in any way except as specifically permitted in writing by the publisher. Any unauthorized distribution or use of this text may be a direct infringement of the author's and publisher's rights, and those responsible may be liable in law accordingly.

For permission to publish, distribute or otherwise reproduce this work, please contact the author at **info@charcoalrecords.co.uk**

Book design by Clare Baggaley

Edited by Lisa Edwards

A CIP catalogue record for this book is available from the British Library.

Standard Hardback - 978-1-7384843-0-0

Collector's Edition - 978-1-7384843-1-7

Printed by Oriental Press, Dubai

MIX
Paper | Supporting responsible forestry
FSC® C004800

To order books, collector's editions, signed LPs or CDs, handwritten lyrics and other merchandise please go to:

www.caradillon.co.uk

CAPTIONS TO PREVIOUS PAGES

The window at Eslin. My mother's childhood home on the mountainside in Glenullin.

On the path leading to Eslin.

for Colm, Noah and Elizabeth

Timing

When everything dies down
Shake the seeds
Let the wind pick them up
Scatter them in the breeze
For no-one is looking about you now
But time will come
Time always does
And you, too, will sprout afresh
From some unexpected corner

———

I wholeheartedly believe that listening to my album, *Coming Home,* will enhance the stories and memories I have written about here. The music lifts my words off the page and becomes an immersive experience.

———

"If writing is the body, then music is the soul."

CARA

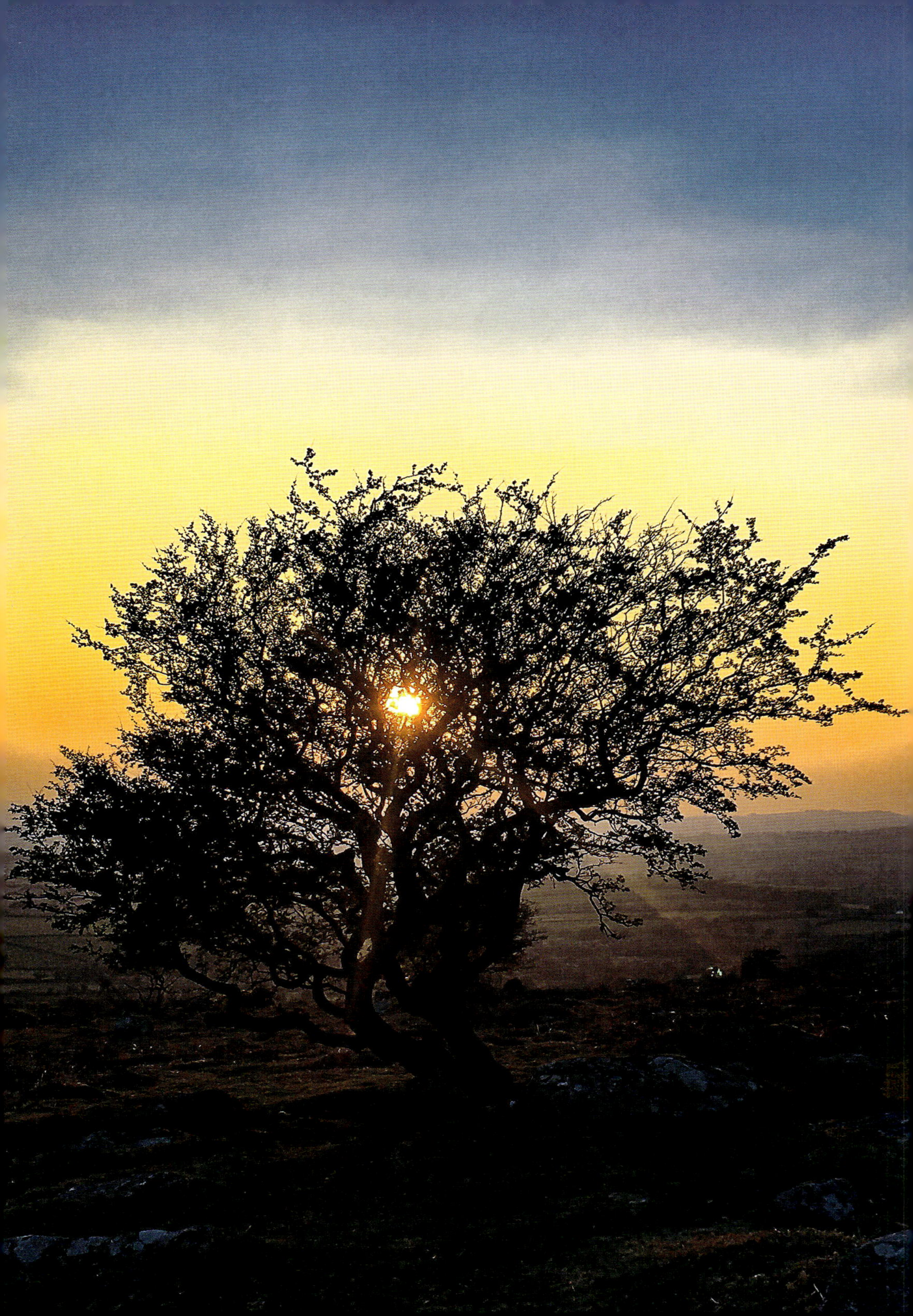

Contents

Introduction 12   Background 18

- Coming Home   22
- Daughter   34
- Mysteries   42
- Inishowen   60
- Clear the Path   74
- Giving   84
- The Cure   94
- White Sheets   110
- Apron Strings   120

Acknowledgments 132   Biography 133   Album Catalogue 134

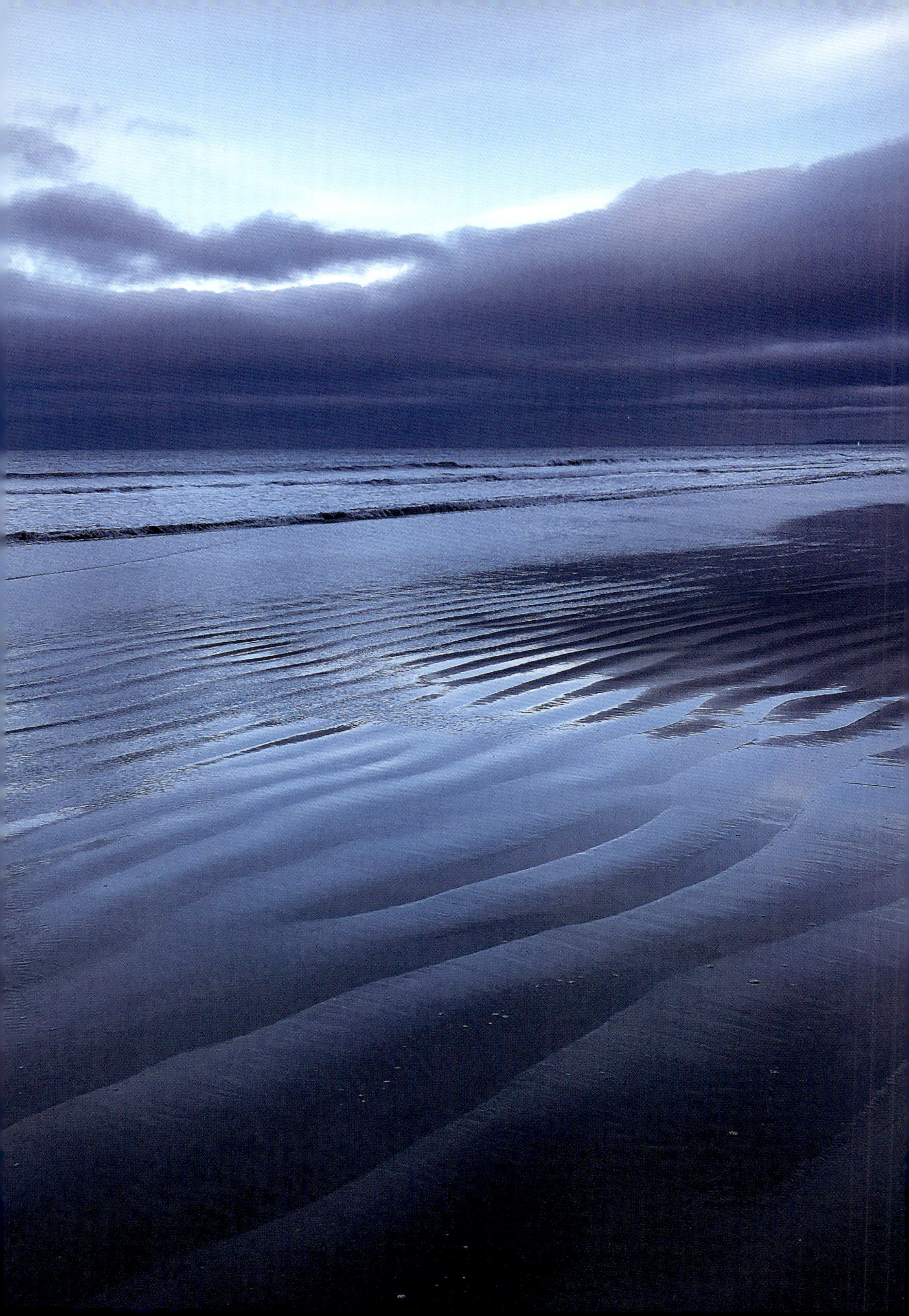

Introduction

Writing a book was certainly never my intention – nor was recording an album of my poetry set to music. The fact is, this project has been the most organic, creative journey I have ever experienced. It is also the most personal and revealing. I could never have imagined that I would be sharing these stories and inviting people to glimpse these private memories. But, I suppose that's what makes it so special. These poems were born out of a time of precious inner peace and entirely without intention. Something I can now look back on and appreciate will, almost certainly, never happen again. The circumstances were rare to say the least.

It all began shortly before the UK went into its first lockdown in 2020. Sam had clocked the inevitability of it all. We first heard news reports while in our New Orleans hotel room, when we were performing there in late January. The spread and the panic following weeks later. Due to me being Type 1 Diabetic, we took the proactive decision to cancel all live shows long before the rest of the industry caught on. We also removed our three children from school three weeks before the official UK lockdown,

PREVIOUS PAGE
Benone Strand at dusk. Over seven miles of beach and an amazing place to lose yourself on the north coast of Co. Derry.

writing to their headmaster to explain our reasons. By the time the rest of the country was in full panic mode, we were already in a relatively calm and established lockdown routine of our own. We'd formed a bubble with my nephew, Odhrán*, who happened to live very close by and was now working from home.

The kids soon settled into their home-learning routines, and Sam became completely obsessed with digging a vegetable patch in anticipation of the end of civilisation. I, on the other hand, found my head slowly emptying. For the first time in God knows how long, I didn't have to think about 'the next thing', whether it was a concert, a recording session, or the countless jobs that constantly need attention when you're a busy, working, mother of three. What happened next was both totally unexpected, and immensely fulfilling.

As the weeks in lockdown passed by, I began waking very early in the mornings and writing; writing without a goal and purely for myself. I've always enjoyed writing, whether it is poetry, songs or stories, but I was *not* a confident writer. In fact, looking at my catalogue of songs, only a small proportion are self-penned. Maybe it's because I've spent so many years singing traditional songs or covers that capture a sentiment or story so much better than I feel I could. Either way, this extraordinary situation provided me with the time to explore the powerful feelings I was having about my home in County Derry, and my family, whom I was clearly unable to visit and didn't know when I would see again. I drifted into a serene headspace, indulging in my own childhood memories, exploring my place in this world and the role I play in my children's lives. Poetry just happened to be

In front of Eslin.

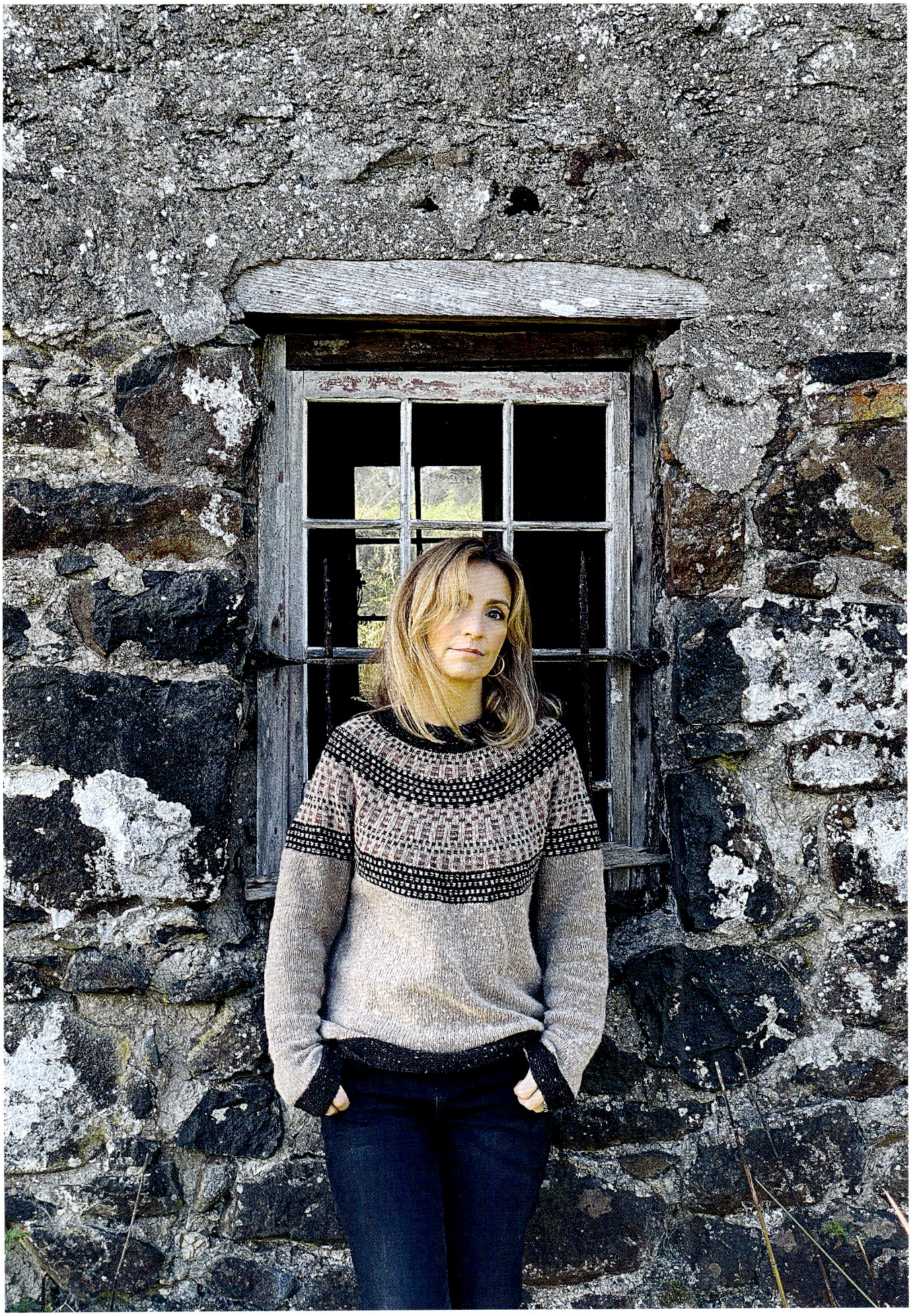

the medium that allowed me to do this best.

For the longest time, Sam and the children were completely unaware I was even writing. When I hit my stride I would wake early, often at dawn (4am) and take myself out to our front garden to write, mug of tea in hand, wrapped in a blanket and listening to the songbirds. We live in the middle of a market town but there were no cars, no trains. I suppose it all sounds a bit too perfect, but that's how it really was. Weeks passed and I was writing passionately about so many memories, different people I love and questions I had.

As I said previously, I'm no writer, but as an artist I quickly recognised this was a rich vein and I knew I was blessed to have time and space to mine it fully. My mother and I would spend hours on the phone talking about her childhood, my late father and her memories. (At the time of writing this she is ninety-two and her long-term memory is as sharp as ever.) It made me appreciate what an important link to the past she is, and what the feeling of 'home' really meant to me and what it might mean to my own children.

I finally built up the courage to read one or two of my poems to Sam and Odhrán. There were watery eyes, a little astonishment and (thankfully) bags of encouragement. At this stage, the 'poems' –I use this word loosely – were in many forms. Some were long streams of consciousness, roughly shaped into mismatched verses; others were neat and fully formed. With a new and welcome confidence, I set about refining the ones that spoke to me the most – maybe about twenty or thirty – at that stage, figuring that maybe I could print them in a pamphlet and sell them at gigs.

Sometime in the autumn, Sam picked up his guitar – as he did most days – and was noodling away in the kitchen. I was preparing something to eat and, without thinking about it, started reciting lines from one of my poems silently in my head while he played. Well, it's not hard to imagine what happened next. It was obvious and inevitable looking back now – but at the time it felt entirely organic and genuinely unforced. It was a process we embarked on slowly and over a long period. The words chose the music and vice versa. During the beginning we certainly didn't think we would be recording them for a 'spoken word' album. But of course, that's exactly what happened. I'm amazed at how each stage of this journey has led to the next without there being a master plan.

Before we began recording the poems, we decided to perform one or two in our set at a few concerts to see if they were even viable. I couldn't have hoped for a better reaction. They felt perfectly at home in amongst the songs I regularly sing, the audience falling silent, allowing our indulgence and immediately relating to the pieces. We were so thankful, for now we had the confidence to move forward and create *Coming Home*, an album that I am immensely proud of.

As we performed more and more of the poems live over the next year or so, it became clear that the stories I told before each piece magnified the experience for the audience in a way I hadn't appreciated before. People would come up to me afterwards to ask me if I was going to write these stories down, that I *should* write these stories down. They shared similar stories about their own children, their own mothers and fathers, and homes they had moved away from. It became obvious there was yet another stage in this journey … and this book is it.

Please don't expect a complete autobiography or for this to be full to the brim of mad stories from the road. These are my personal inspirations and memories that led and relate to each of the poems from *Coming Home* as well as a few lyrics and other pieces that I feel are particularly relevant. All the pictures are family photos or have been taken by me, Sam or Odhrán.**.

*pronounced "Oran"
** unless credited otherwise

Background

M any of you reading this will already be familiar with my wee corner of the world. Throughout this book, I delve deeper, including stories and memories about various members of my family, and places that are important to me. However, I thought it would be worthwhile to provide a short description of

My mother and father, Teresa and Frank Dillon, taken sometime in the 1950s.

them here before you read on.

I was born in Dungiven, which is a small town in County Derry, in the North of Ireland, a place where culture, history and identity are bound together with the dramatic landscape. I've only ever known its people to be fiercely proud and incredibly supportive.

I am the youngest of six – Anne, Mary, Joan and Emma (twins) and Francis (the only boy) – and it's no surprise that I have countless aunts, uncles and cousins. My mother and father were both born and raised in Glenullin, a small, remote area at the very north-eastern edge of the Sperrin Mountains.

My father, Frank, was born in 1921 and my mother, Teresa, in 1931, and both lived very rural lives until moving to the town shortly after getting married. The cottages they were raised in only had a couple of rooms in which their entire families lived and were located less than half a mile from each other. They were typical whitewashed, single-storey cottages with thatched roofs and no running water or electricity – the focus of each cottage being the open hearth with a turf fire. Their stories have linked me with a past that, in some ways, wouldn't be out of place in the nineteenth century. I realise what an extraordinary privilege it has been to be so deeply connected to that history and to the land my ancestors worked … but more about that later.

Me, aged six.

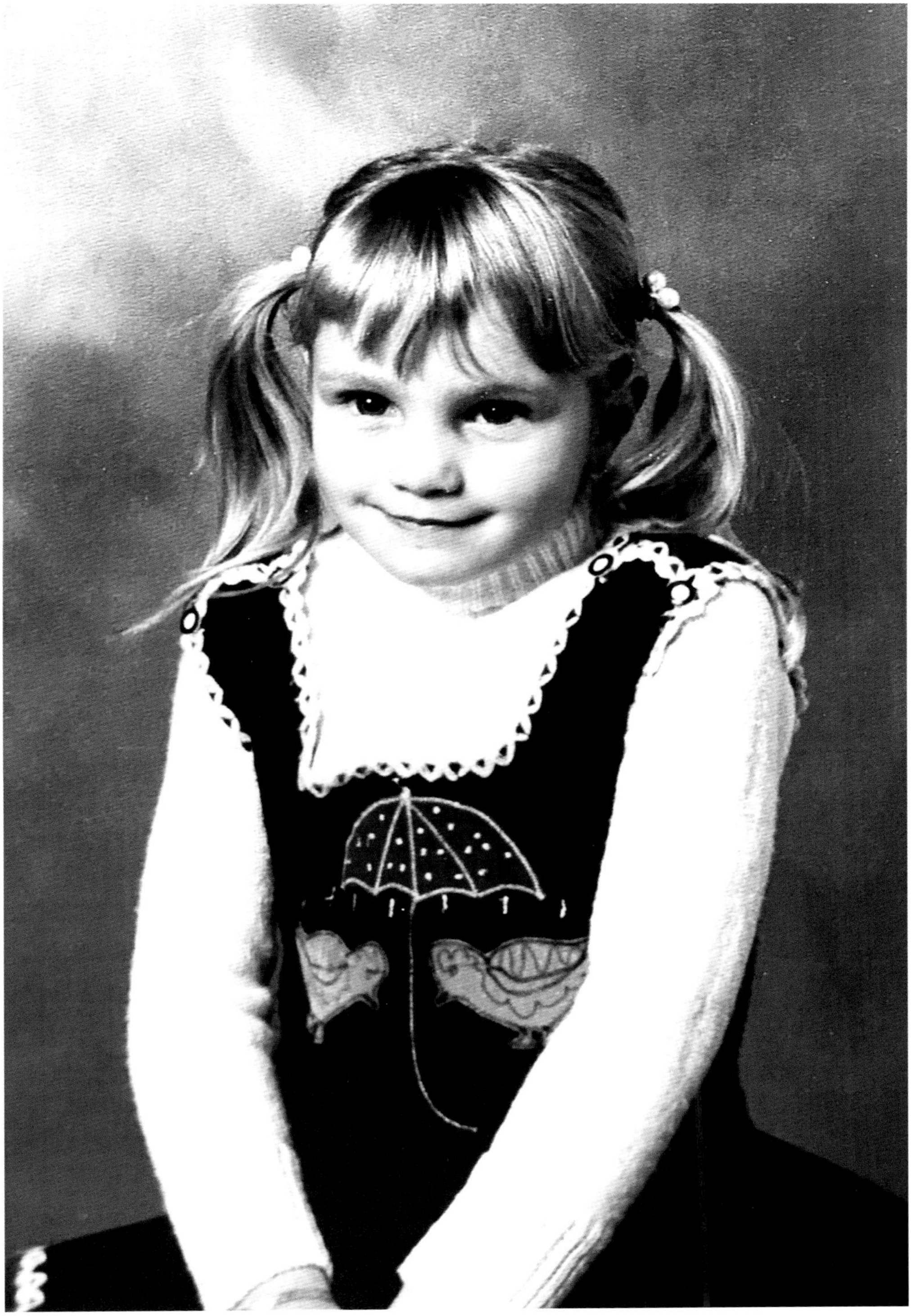

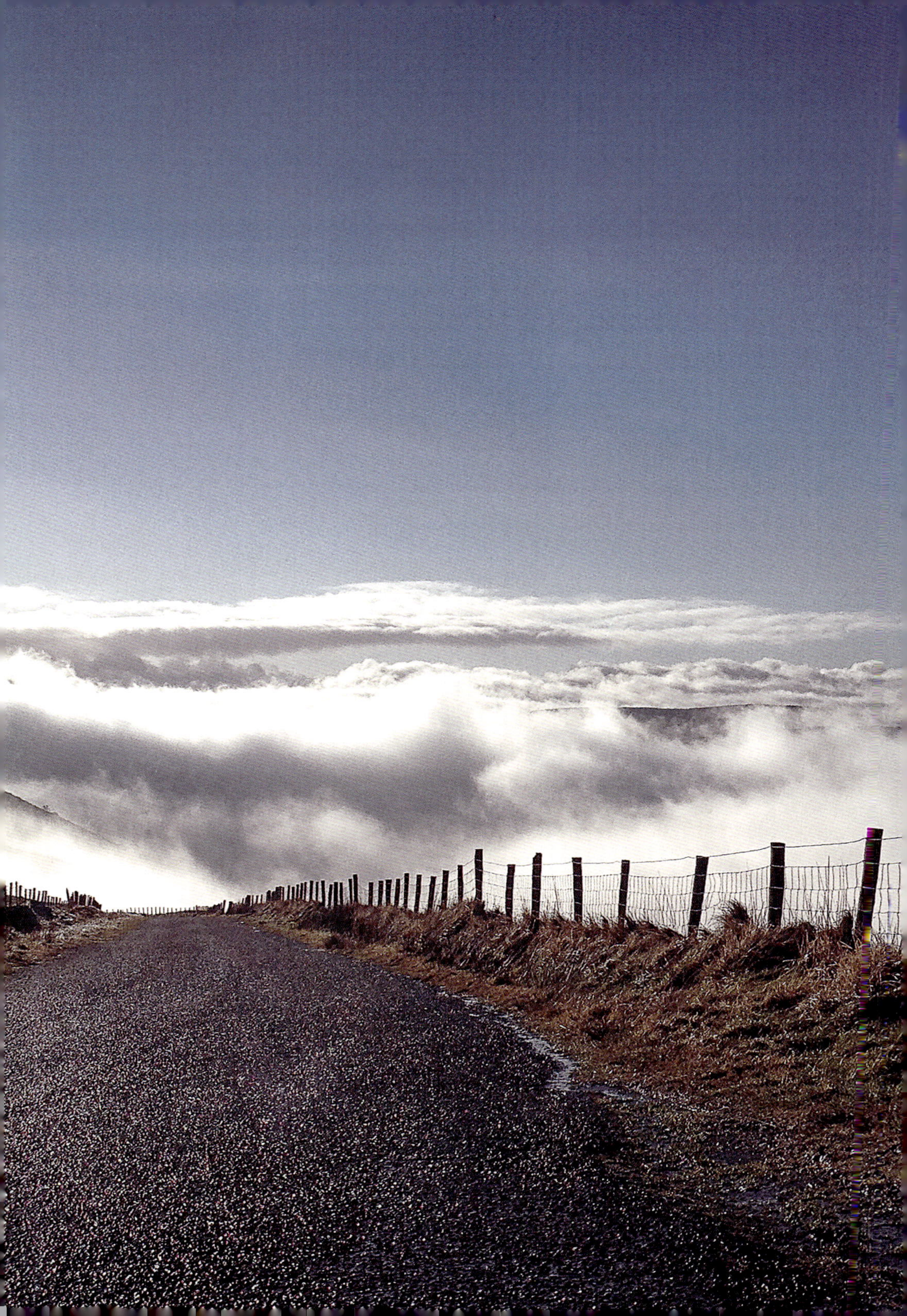

Coming Home

Are you still coming home? When are you coming home? Both questions should probably be written on my gravestone, for I'm asked this pretty much weekly by my family, and I'll never get tired of it. It's something many people reading this may well relate to. It can be one of the most reassuring questions I can think of; the feeling that the people I love most are wanting to know when we can be together again. But it can also be a complicated question for someone like me, who lives and works far away from home.

In 2002 and 2003, I was deep in a continuous cycle of arrivals and departures from tours and concerts from all over the world. My career was suddenly taking off and I was very busy indeed. Together with Sam, I performed hundreds of shows a year and made countless TV and radio appearances. The year 2002 ended on a particular high when Sam and I were married after returning from

From the top of Benbradagh, looking down towards Dungiven which is hidden by low cloud.

an intense tour of Germany, Belgium and The Netherlands.

They say that things must always have balance, an equilibrium, and so I found that just as my career began to take off, another area of my life weighed heavily on the scales. I can name a few times in my life when this has happened, when a big readjustment was imminent. But I also know it's not that you need to deny the great things from happening – just knowing that the pendulum is swinging is life's inescapable way of teaching us what's really important. Although there was much happiness and excitement at that time, there was also immense stress and sadness. My father wasn't well. In fact, he declined rapidly soon after our wedding, almost like he was giving one final push to walk me, his youngest daughter, up the aisle.

Lots of things were changing fast: the same house I'd left to do my first proper gigs together with my teenage friends ten years previously now had an enormous sleeper bus parked outside it with the cream of the Irish music scene onboard. I was taking part in the national tour of the tenth anniversary of *A Woman's Heart* (the biggest-selling album in Irish chart history).

It was absolutely great *craic* and amazing to be performing in some of the largest theatres in Ireland, but as each day went on, I'd call Mammy to hear how Daddy

Outside McReynolds' Bar on Dungiven main street. One of many great pubs in the town.

was and it seemed that he was getting progressively worse. The only real comfort was that I was in Ireland and not a long flight away if something bad did happen. The gigs were sold out every night and I was on stage with the legendary Irish female artists I had grown up inspired by – Mary Black, Dolores Keane and Sharon Shannon – and yet all the time I felt that inevitable pendulum swinging.

There was a moment on that tour that I re-live over and over again, and I still cannot get over the kindness shown to me and absolutely hilarity of the situation. We were due to perform in the prestigious Waterfront Hall in Belfast. On our way up the road from the West Coast of Ireland, we travelled towards Dungiven from Derry, when Maura O'Connell had a quiet word with Mick (the bus driver) and we found ourselves hanging a left at the top of the town and pulling up right outside my parents' home. When you're travelling on a tour bus you share in each other's ups and downs so the ladies knew pretty well the situation was bleak. My father's health was fragile to say the least, and they had allowed me to take a moment to run in and be with him – gig be damned! In fact, they'd wanted to come in and sing him a song, but I knew things were way beyond that stage.

Now, Mammy, being a fan of these ladies herself, was absolutely mortified that I hadn't called ahead so that she could get the kettle on and have the tay made. "God, Cara, you're not leaving them on the bus… This is awful!"

As I sat there with my daddy for those precious few moments, those songbirds of Ireland, with talent beyond words, stretched their legs in the road in front of our house, my daddy telling me there was plenty of brandy in the cupboard and that I should make sure to give them all a good sup.

When you move away from your homeland, I believe you see things with different eyes, the changes that time brings, how nothing stays the same for too long. Nieces and nephews grow in between visits, members of the community pass on and are then brought back to life in memories, stories and sometimes songs. Being the youngest meant I had seen our house empty one by one, as each of us packed up and left home ... only for it to fill up again later with grandchildren and then empty once more. So

My father, Frank. Taken in my sister, Mary's, kitchen in Dungiven. Sometime in the early 1990s.

now, when I come home, I find my mother in her nineties, wondering to herself, "Where has the time gone?"

Coming home for me has always been a coming back to the source – the source of who I am and what made me. My poem was initially inspired by my memories of a tour in New Zealand, Australia and Singapore in 2003. After the initial excitement of being on the other side of the world for festivals and TV and radio appearances, I had a sharp shock when I realised just how far away from home I really was. I was in a hotel in New Plymouth, Taranaki, and it was before I had my own mobile phone, so in a desperate moment, I just went ahead and reversed the charges from my hotel room to call home and speak to my parents.

My father came on the line and I heard his familiar voice ask me if I was okay. I said I was "wile homesick," choking back tears, to which he replied, "Well, if you're feeling that bad would you not just come on home?"

It made me laugh... He had a way of simplifying my problems. But the more he said to "come on home" the more I told him I needed to stay and that I couldn't let anyone down. I can't stress how that phone call really settled me. It connected me in that moment with my family and home. Even now, whenever I feel a little lost or low, I pick up the phone and speak to one of my own back in Dungiven and it settles me beyond measure.

I suppose it's part and parcel of the job, it's the price you pay – the travel, the distances and an endless aching heart for home – made all the worse when something is wrong. I often think about that feeling of belonging to a place, to a family and how important it is, that knowing you are always loved and welcome. It's the stability of it all that is so important, especially for a touring musician. I know that Sam feels it too and I hope that we are creating that security for our own family, even as we continue to come and go.

My very first trip home after my father passed away in October 2003 was hard; I knew everything was profoundly different, things could never be the same: that first flight home, the drive over the dramatic Glenshane pass, all the while knowing that Mammy would now be stood all alone, arms outstretched – ready to welcome me home.

Just some of the letters written to me by my mother when I first left home, and even though I spoke with her almost every day on the phone, I always looked forward to her weekly reports of our family's life.

OVERLEAF
A bookshelf in my home, which is full of pictures of our children, my family, Sam's family, and my first pair of shoes.

29 ● Coming Home

IRISH MUSIC AWARDS
2004
BEST IRISH FEMALE SINGER
CARA DILLON

Seamus Heaney Opened Ground: Poems 1966–1996
Folk and Traditional Music of the Western Continents
NETTL
The Cloudspot
COLLECTED POEMS W. B. YEATS
Ed. AUGUSTINE MARTIN
A NATURAL HISTORY OF THE SENSES
Diane Ackerman
THE POETRY OF W.B. YEATS
The Stone Fiddle
PADDY TUNNEY
Folklore of the Ulster People by Sheila St.Clair
EILEEN DUNLOP
JAMES JOYCE Ulysses
THE NEW POETRY
MICHAEL HULSE, DAVID KENNEDY & DAVID MORLEY
Ireland
A Novel
FRANK DELANEY
MORE IRISH
JAMES JOYCE

Coming Home

We haven't seen you in a while,
Sitting cross-legged on the floor,
Fine hair static,
Eyes lost in a dream.

We'll bring you back one day
To the wind and the rain
And the snow, and the River Roe,
And these walls you know.
And you know
The smell of the sea will bring you round.
And we'll dig out those songs you used to sing,
And the books tidied away now,
For it's nothing but joy they bring,
And you'll scatter their words to the wind.

And you'll scatter their words to the wind.
It's been too long now,
Won't you come on home?
And though it seems like time stands still,
There's always more to come.
Won't you come on home?

We'll colour your thoughts.
We'll listen to you,
Chase the shadows,
Lose sleep over you,
And we'll stand up for you.
For no one knows you like we do.
No one knows you like we do.
Would you not come on home now?
I'm waiting on you.

―――

His Hands

When I see him now
The light is softer and blurred.
Sawdust falls from his shoulders
And settles on the floor like illuminous gold
And you're happy at it again,
Never as happy.
Sawing and crafting
Thumbnail, marking the boards.
The curls of wood you planed
Proving to me over and over again
That everything's possible but nothing's straightforward,
Not even a plank of wood.
Tongue and groove
Side by side we stand,
Your pencil tucked behind your ear,
Mine firmly in my hand.

―――

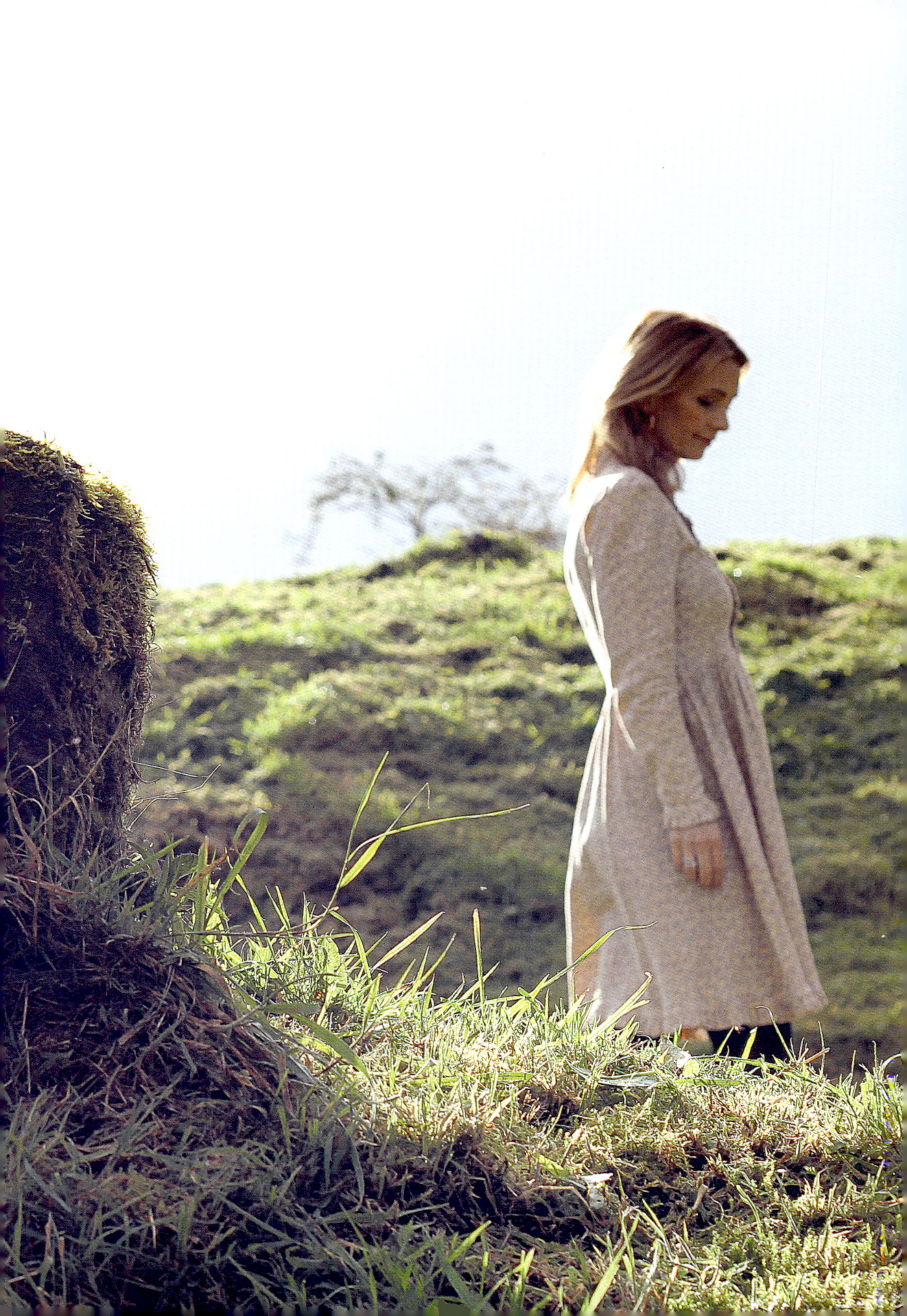

Daughter

Thank you for the beautiful moments that have allowed me to write this book. Thank you for this moment I have found myself in, as my hand glides effortlessly over a page, for I am not a writer. I am nobody but myself. The life that flows inside me did not begin the second I was conceived, nor will it end when I die. Incredible things have been bubbling throughout the generations, long before I came to light. But I now find myself able to understand my place in this world better than at any time in my life.

It's not quite clear to me when I finally open my eyes. Why was I alone in a room and what exactly had happened? I turned my head slowly to see two small photos by my hospital bedside: pictures of two tiny doll-like babies attached to tubes, wearing masks to breathe like they've come from a different place in this universe and they don't know how to survive. Where were they and where was Sam?

Just then, the door opened and in came a lovely lady called Mary. She had tears in her eyes and she called me her "little flower". She told me that she'd just helped

In the grounds of the old Priory on the outskirts of Dungiven.

deliver my twenty-six-week-old babies. She went on to say that in her whole life of midwifery, she had never seen a baby born still inside its perfectly intact bubble. She said it was the most beautiful thing she'd ever seen and that all who were present during the emergency birth didn't want that rare moment to end. They looked on in wonder, not wanting to break the amniotic sac. The baby looking so content, so perfectly happy and safe. She says she needs me to take this picture with me forever in my heart, for the doctors are now coming in with some very difficult news. I was told it was unlikely that Noah and Colm would survive, and if they did, there would likely be many complications. Mary also told me that it's widely known throughout parts of the world that an 'en caul' birth bestows the baby with the greatest of luck and even special powers. Now, this is just what I needed to hear. This is what I continued to hold on to with every fibre in my body.

As I write this now, that chapter of my life feels like a dream. And yet I can hear every beep of the CPAP machine, every hushed conversation with doctors standing over the incubators, and feel every blessed moment that I got to cradle my babies, skin-on-skin like little kangaroos. They weighed 2lb 10oz and 2lb 13oz when they were born on 17 November 2006, which is actually a pretty good weight considering. We brought them home with us on 17 February 2007 (their actual due date). It has been the most incredible and often indescribable journey I could ever have wished or hoped for, since they are my two suns. On 12 October 2010, my daughter, Elizabeth, was born in the very same room the boys came into this world, but, thankfully, under very different circumstances. She is my moon.

My daughter, Elizabeth, and me in the fields near our home in Somerset.

Coming Home   36

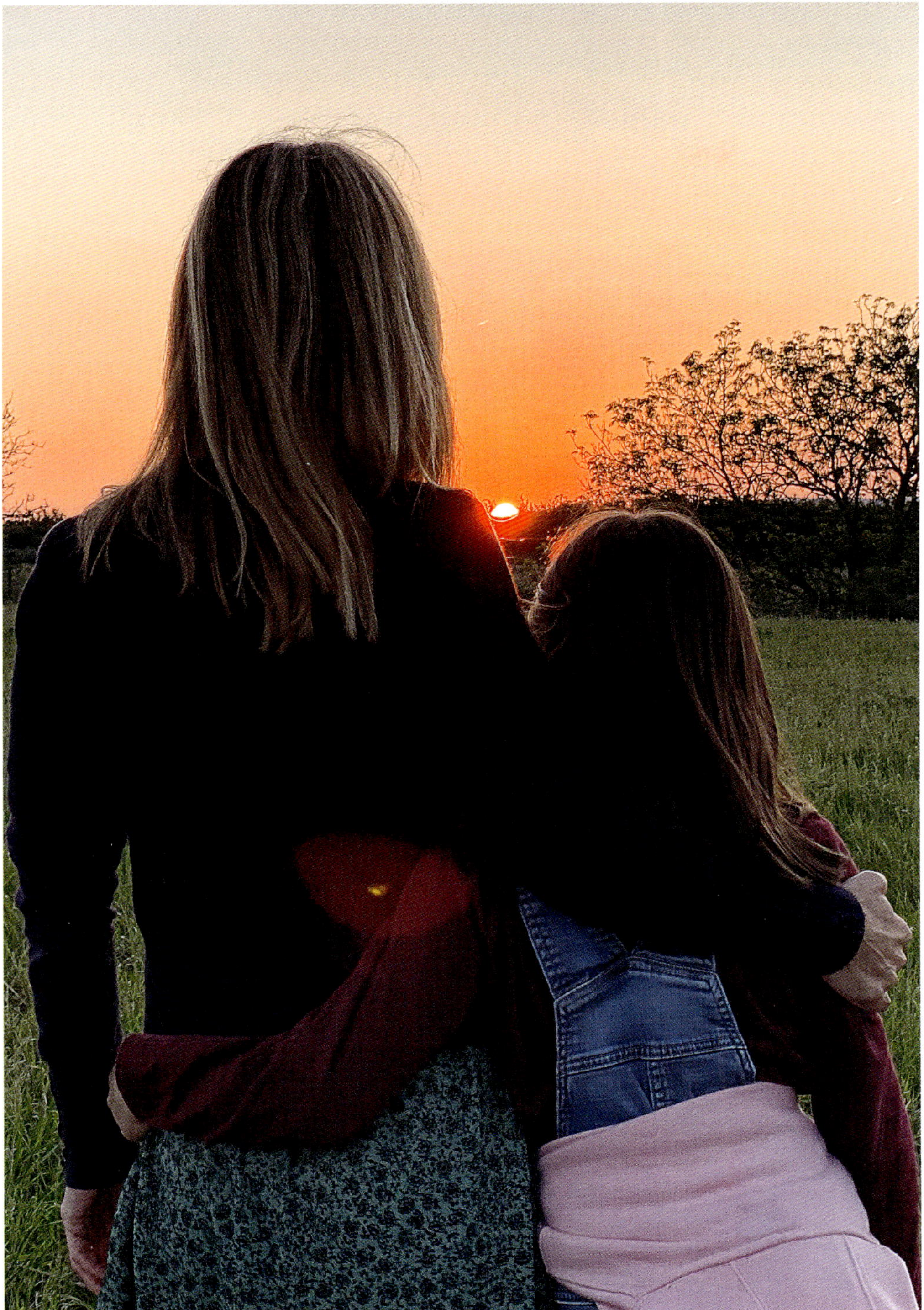

My children have illuminated my life in ways I could never imagine. They are all things, all at once. They are what makes me strong and vulnerable at the same time. They are my link to the past and my hope for the future and it is for them that I wrote these poems, and now this book. We inherit so much of who we are, but the potential we carry within us is enormous. We may just be the one that breaks the mould, that creates a spark, that mends and fixes broken family relationships; the one that defies our family's medical history, eradicating a whole lineage of

My great grandmother, Brigid O'Mullan, along with (l-r) my mother and her sisters, Susan, May and Bridie. Taken sometime in the mid 1930s.

disease from a single cell the moment we are born. This is our time. It is our moment to shine.

The sun doesn't shine differently on different people. We're all just here waiting to step out of a shadow and find a little ray of light that will illuminate our true selves. And we're not alone. We're constantly reminded of this when we see our grandmother's eyes looking back at us through our daughters, or when our children discover a skill or talent that comes easily to them, only to learn that it was in the family a few generations ago.

I think about my own journey so far as a woman, how I am still learning so much about myself through my daughter, how she teaches me so much. She has brought with her the spirit and resilience of *her* ancestors. She has sat by my mother's side and listened to her yarns about her life long ago and has learnt to be still in these moments, to absorb and digest, for she knows they're important. She's sat beside my mother-in-law, Joy, and listened to her infectious laugh while watching her effortlessly handle a house full of dynamic male personalities. She's been at my side when I've had diabetic hypos on her birthday, knowing exactly what to do to help. She's sat in a room with my sisters, wide-eyed, as they crack on, including her in their circle of trust, showing that there is unity and solidarity among us, in spite of us living very different lives.

We are stronger because of the unwavering strength of our mothers and daughters. Eventually, we all have our own stories to tell, our own role models and our own desires to find and speak up for who we are. But we also need to speak up for those who have gone before us, who've been waiting for us for a long time now.

Daughter

She's got his eyes and my smile,
Her nose and her fine hair
And hands like theirs.
Stitched together at the seams
With bits and bobs from old pictures and dreams.

But her soul goes deeper than them all.
For she was born with a veil over her face,
Drowning in luck;
Sent to navigate the space between worlds
With a wisdom and knowledge she could never understand.
We've been waiting for you for a long time.

And she's picture-perfect
As she stands upon the moss,
Green like her eyes and she, too, will become it.
She feels the sounds from underground,
The bass of a new earth thumping through her rattling bones,
And she turns her palms towards the sun.
We've been waiting for you for a long time.

Hope of all
Wonder seeker
Morning star
Star gazer
Light of hope
Daughter of the sea
Little bird
Wild fire
Little flower
Warrior of truth
Torch of hope
Gracious gift
We've been waiting for you for a long time.

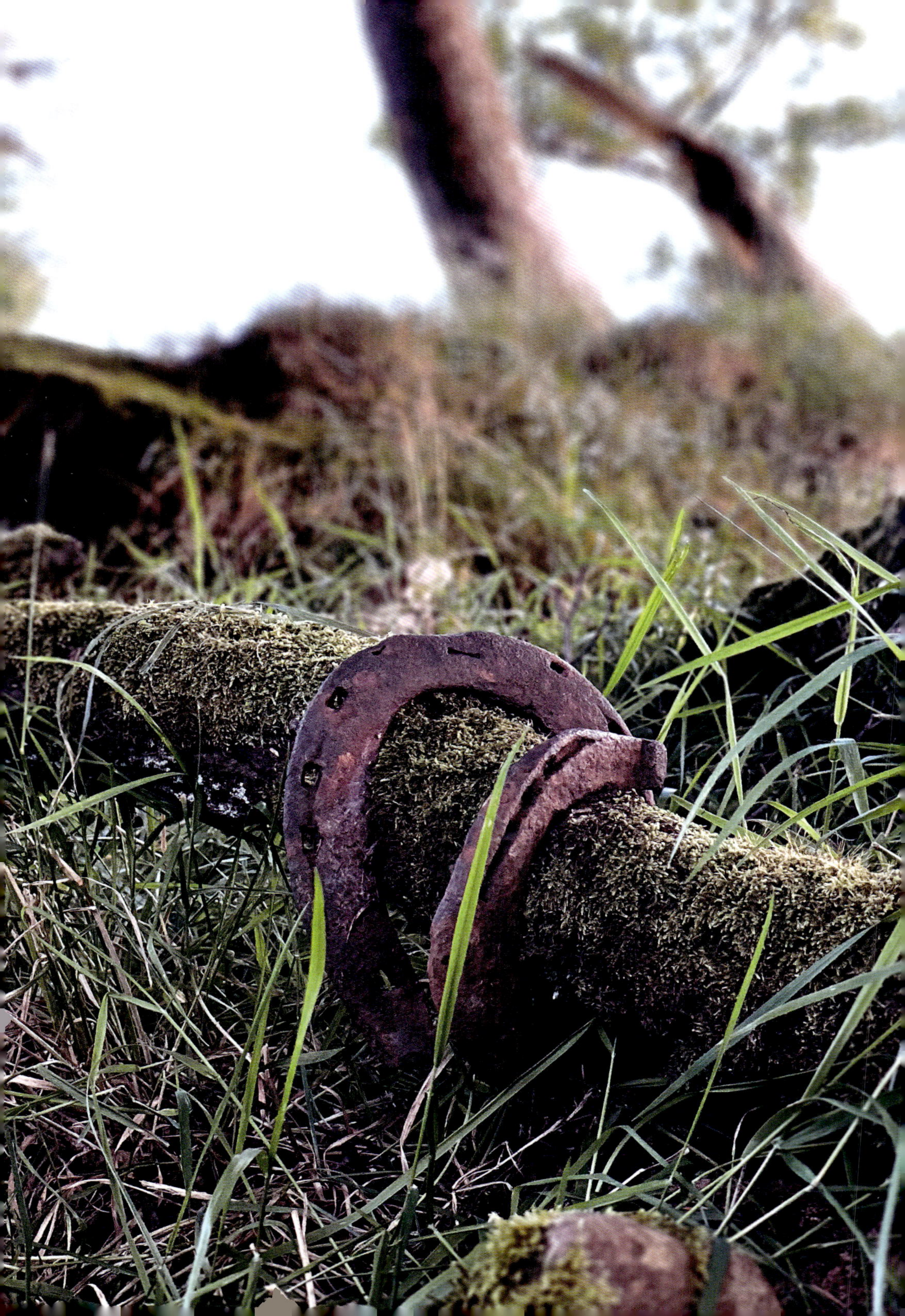

Mysteries

●

Although I never met my grandparents from either side of the family, I've always felt a deep connection to them. In more recent years, I became haunted by an image of Elizabeth Dillon (Lizzie), my 'Granny Bing'. She's standing by a half-closed stable door outside her cottage, one hand resting on the bottom half, hair scraped back in a bun and her eyes searching for me. She's thirty-eight years old in this vision, the same age she became a widow, and she seems to be trying to tell me something. I can feel her warmth and her love for me and I feel an overwhelming sense of responsibility to tell her story. Her life was hard and as far as I'm aware, it became much harder after her husband died, leaving her – a young woman – with a family of four to rear.

At the end of this short, narrow lane in the glen is The Bing, the cottage where my father was born and raised. It sits in a field on the side of the mountain, and benefits from the welcome shelter of a shallow valley. There, you'll find the sound of a babbling stream where my daddy, as a young boy, caught freshwater trout with his bare hands.

Kate and Fanny, the two farm horses at Eslin, had their discarded shoes hung high on a branch by the farrier to keep them out of the way. Over time, the branch grew around the shoes, making their removal impossible. Eventually, the branch rotted and fell from the tree, only to be discovered by Sam just a few years ago.

Later, the fish would be fried in butter over the open fire. My auntie and mother refer to this method of fishing for trout as "ginling". It was also along this remote lane that my grandfather would go wandering in a 'daze' after he'd suffered a stroke. When it was his turn, my father was charged with staying awake at night to mind his own sick father, making sure he didn't wander off or drown in the stream. When he was eleven years old, my father breathed a sigh of relief when the old man died, but also felt a hateful blend of guilt and shame when death finally came to take his father, for now he could finally sleep uninterrupted and without worry.

It was from The Bing that my grandmother left to walk

The old stove still sits in the kitchen of The Bing, my father's childhood home in Glenullin.

the five miles to Garvagh, a year to the day that her husband died, to buy herself a lilac blouse to wear for the second year following his death. The change from black to lilac symbolised the emotional journey from grief and sadness to acceptance, showing her coming out of mourning and continuing with life. When Lizzie was on her way home from Garvagh, on a corner of this very road, she was teased by a local man; his ill-judged comment inferring that she "couldn't wait for the year to end so that she could get on with her life and marry again". Now, pride being such a powerful motivator: she duly returned the blouse and from that day on she continued to wear nothing but black until the day she died.

I often think about the words we choose and the effect they can have on others, they can be truly life-changing – literally! Back then, in small-town land, community was important, but reputation was absolutely everything. Folks had very little and yet they could be so judgmental of their neighbours. With time on their hands, a few idle tongues could cause a world of damage. Mammy often used to say about that time, "You had tuppence ha'penny looking down on tuppence."

The following poem is the very first I wrote from this collection. We didn't record it – it hasn't found it's music yet. But I needed Elizabeth's story to be told and for her to not be forgotten. She lives through me in the DNA that we share, linked forever.

38, Lilac Blouse

Birds   Water   Bee

I heard your whisper
So I walked up the lane to where you sat
For years
You knew my step coming to your door,
You knew
It's you I called my daughter for

Wood   Smoke   Ash

And I watched your hands busy themselves,
You tidying those twin-shelves with pride.
Displaying your life, only to you.

38
Widowed
Back skirt
Lilac blouse
Mourning mellowed by the stream

A year to the day you chose pride.
Grief measured by the blackness of cloth,
Judged by the best and the worst of them
And they thought they knew you
What did they know?

You're not so far from me now.

Less than half a mile away across the fields from The Bing, my mother, Teresa, grew up in a cottage called Eslin. As a small child, she remembers her family sitting one evening as they usually would, with the oil lamp burning and the fire going, when they heard footsteps coming up the lane and right on up to the door. Now, Eslin is at least a mile up its own dirt track from the road, with just the wild, exposed mountain beyond … no one just 'happens' to come up to the cottage.

Her father called out, "Who goes there? Throw in your cap!" It was a traditional welcome that took place before someone set foot through the door, a way of identifying a visitor.

But this time no one came in…no hat was thrown… the door remained shut.

They listened in silence as they heard the footsteps walk on past the window and on up towards the mountain. Mary (my grandmother) insisted that they all fall to their

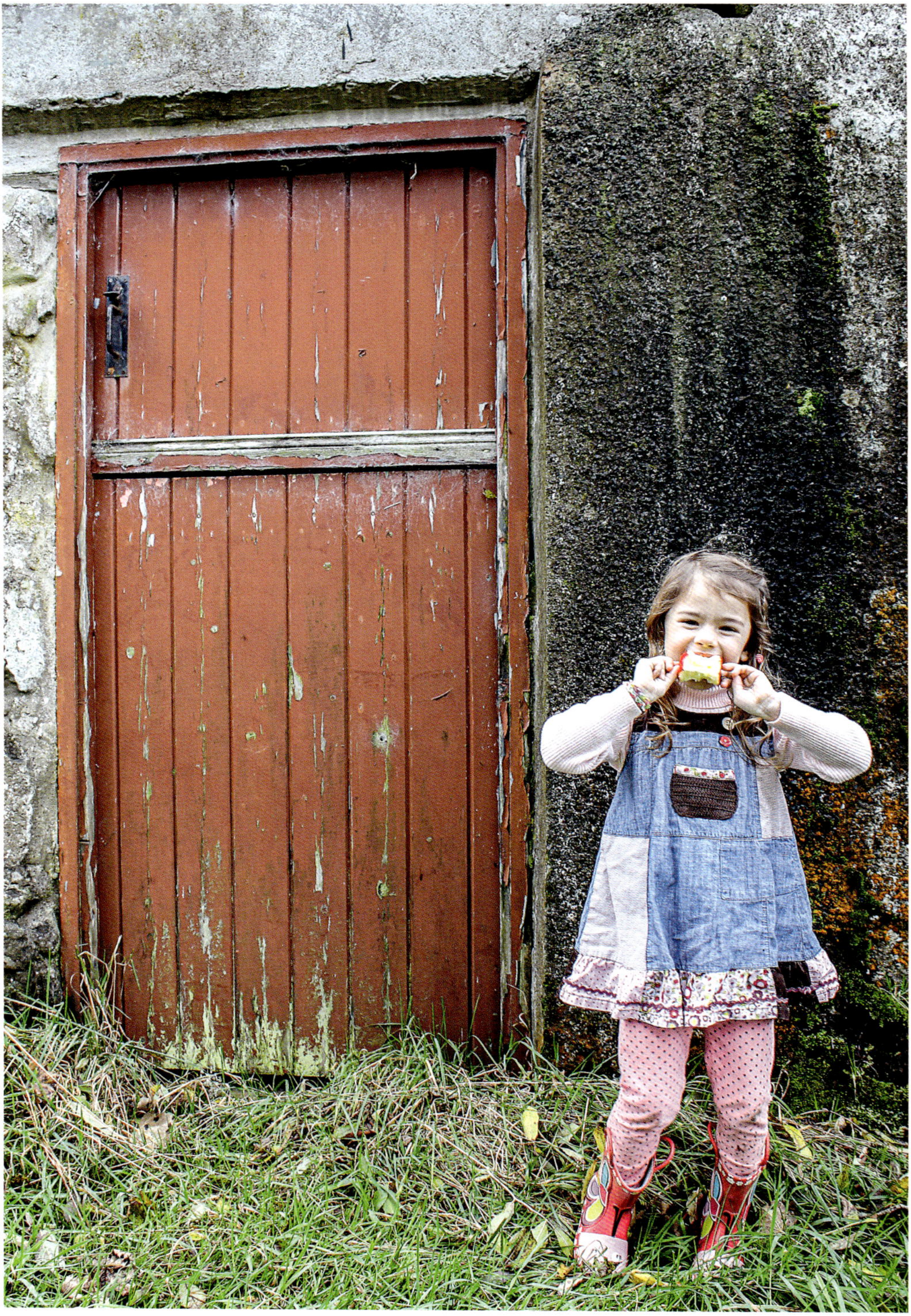

knees at once and say a decade of the rosary for Uncle Dan who, she was certain, had just died in America. Mary told my mother and her siblings that his soul was returning to let them know he was leaving this world and that they should pray.

I can't imagine what those wee girls and boys were thinking in that dramatic moment but, not long after this, a telegram arrived with the news Dan was dead and had (as my mother recalls) passed away on the very same night they had heard the footsteps and knock at the door. This story gives me shivers, even now.

I grew up singing countless songs about Irish emigrants. In fact, one of the first songs I ever learned was "The Winding River Roe", a song based on an old letter from a local man who emigrated to America and longed for his home in The Benedy (just outside Dungiven). His wish when he finally departed this world was to return once more … a story almost identical to the one my mother told me about Uncle Dan. I have always felt this same powerful pull, being drawn to family and my home. I suppose we Irish are renowned the world over for our ability to talk up our motherland to mythical proportions.

My daughter Elizabeth in front of Elizabeth Dillon's door at The Bing.

OVERLEAF
In front of Eslin, in the sunshine.

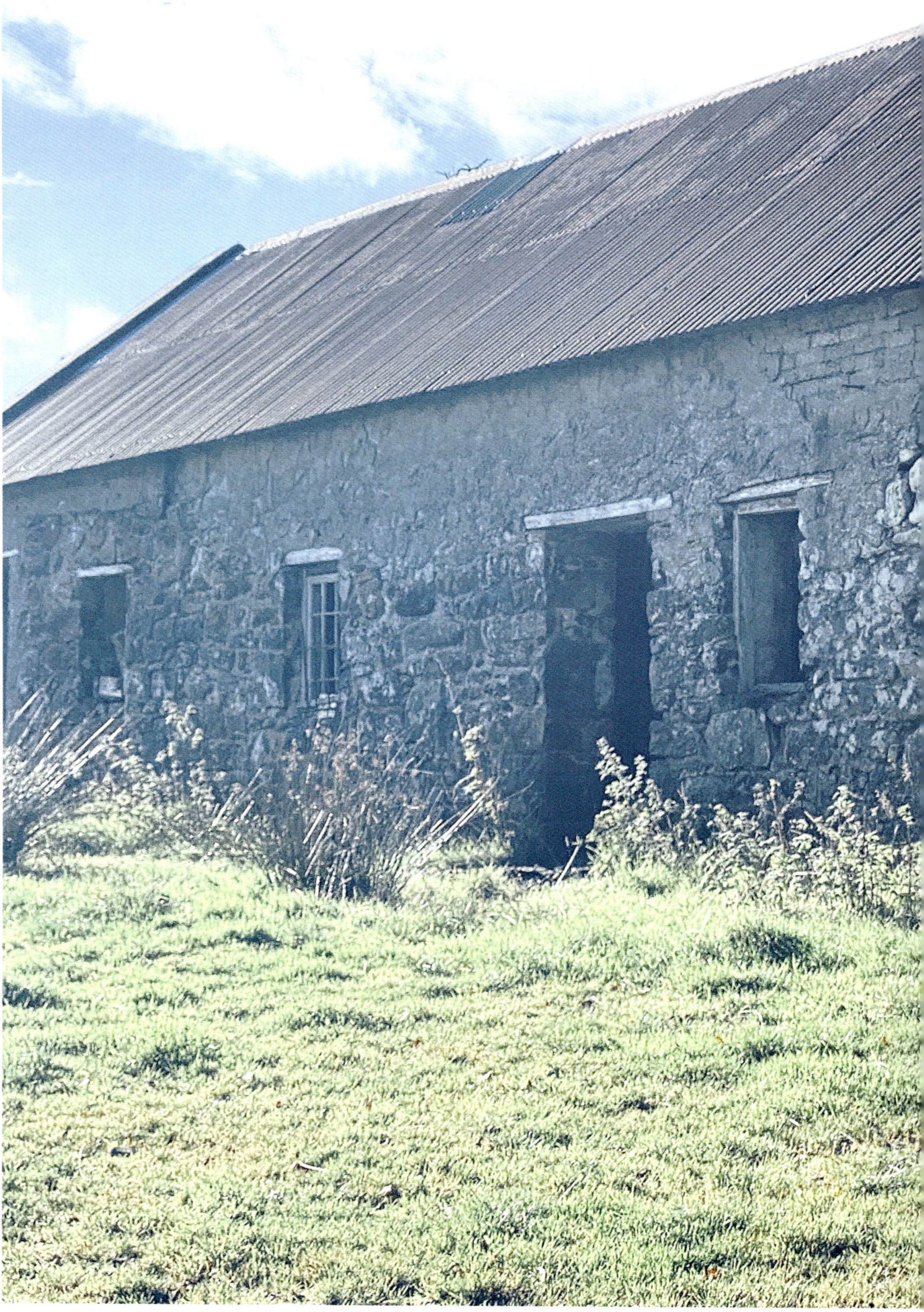

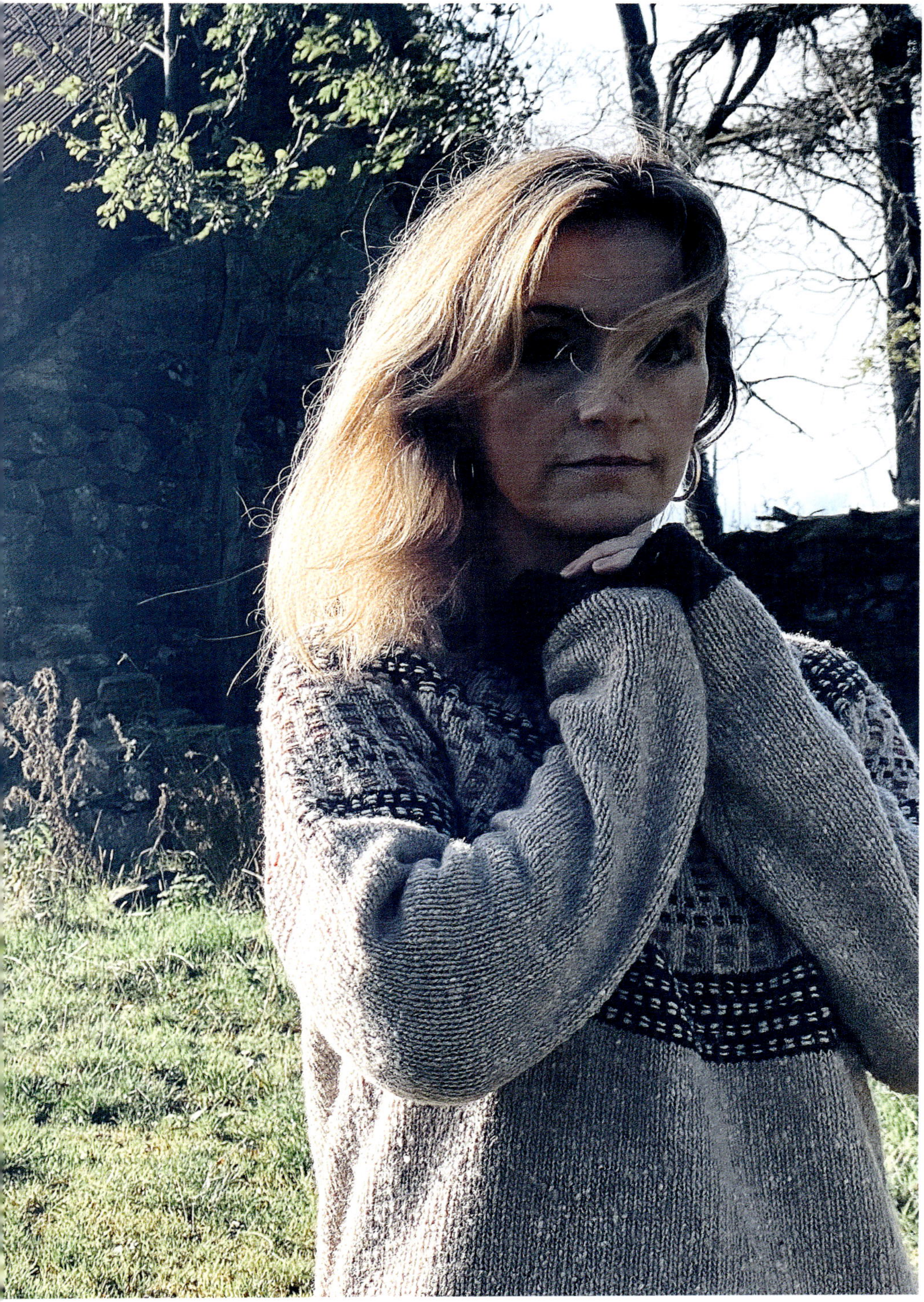

The Winding River Roe

Some poets sing of a noble king,
Or of a sweetheart fair.
Some tell a tale of ships that sail
With treasures rich and rare.
But my humble pen still drifts again
To scenes of long ago,
Across the sea to The Benedy
And the winding River Roe.

Right well do I remember now
Those happy childhood days.
And the times I had when just a lad,
On Carn's lovely braes.
And when my mind is thus inclined
No other joys I know,
For my heart remains on the verdant plains
Near the winding River Roe.

Benbradagh's crown o'er Dungiven town,
Is still within my view,
And The Benedy glen I worshipped then
Still lives in memory too.
The beautiful scene of Cashel Green
Still haunts wherever I go.
And in all my dreams, I see it seems
The winding River Roe.

If fortunes smiles on me awhile,
I would cross the sea again,
And all these years of toil and tears
Will be forgotten then.
And when at last my life has passed,
Contentedly I'll go,
Across the sea to The Benedy
And the winding River Roe.

―――

Traditional; appears on Cara's album, *Sweet Liberty*, released 2003

I often think about the oil lamps that burned back in the glen where my ancestors came from; the conversations that took place, the silence, the prayers and the space given to think and to know and connect in a way that we have mostly forgotten.

Silence has become a welcome friend of mine these days. There is so much noise and distraction that I have found it essential to step outside of myself and just be. I find myself writing and listening by candlelight more and more; I feel it brings respect and reverence to a situation, its gentle flame in such contrast to the bright lights of our home. It's my way of escaping to an inner place and, with its light as gentle company, how a lot of these poems and stories have come to light, so to speak.

Now, where I'm from, a blessed candle is an essential item to have in the home, being brought out in times of need: births, deaths, illnesses, exams, job interviews, travelling relatives, a means to gain the Spirit, and also reassurance. When my sister, Emma, went into labour, her twin sister Joan who was thousands of miles away in America called home with terrible pains in her stomach, completely unaware her sister's baby was coming. And when Joan went on to have her first child, Emma also felt the labour pangs while at work in Derry. No doubt the blessed candle was lit on both these days. In fact, when I went into premature labour with our twin boys, I heard that a prayer circle had begun 'back home' in Ireland. News that our wee babies might not make it travelled quickly and the

One of the many candles that burn in my home.

Coming Home ● 54

community sent word out that for twenty-four hours, prayers would be said continuously throughout the North of Ireland for them.

Some time later, I heard that people from Belfast to Donegal, Fermanagh to County Tyrone, had stayed up through the night praying. There were people that I'd never met before and might never meet, but they prayed when they heard the news. Even now, over sixteen years later, when I go home to perform, Sam and I always have audience members waiting to speak to us after the concert, inquiring after the "wee twins". The boys are not boys anymore but tall young men who recently sat their first big exams – my blessed candle was lit every day for them too.

I've always been fascinated by the instincts we have, the compelling feelings we just can't explain and how we appear to remain connected to loved ones on a spiritual and even physical level. I firmly believe that within our busy minds we need to find more space to focus on what we truly know and that maybe other influences are sadly being drowned out by the cacophony of our modern lives.

My poem "Mysteries", is not really based on one particular experience, but rather an abundance of knowings. Like when I think about someone out of the blue and in that very moment, they ring my phone or like the time a robin hopped into my brother's kitchen through an open door, right before my father died … a forewarning?

The last occasion I spent alone with my father before he passed was when I took him in a wheelchair to a large open field beside the hospital he was in. He clearly wasn't well, being depressed and wanting desperately to come home. I reckoned that a breath of fresh air would help us both and decided in a moment of clean madness to try and

Spring flowers from the garden on my kitchen dresser in the month of May. I absolutely love flowers ... and vintage china.

get a laugh out of him. I ran off around the field chasing a single black crow while he watched on. I knew that ultimately his situation was hopeless, but eventually he lifted his head up to watch me, mustering the strength to say, "Your head's away with it, young cutty," and we both laughed. I just needed to try and lift his spirits, help pick him up a bit: the ridiculous situation and time we shared that day helped us both to take a deep breath and briefly reset, for we knew time was running out. I hadn't spoken a word of this story or told anyone about this moment (not even Sam) as it seemed so simple and unimportant – just the two of us, a father and daughter, a field and a black bird.

Fast forward eight years and one morning I was driving our twin boys to school (then aged five). Noah asked Colm to tell me about the dream he'd had the night before, and Colm recalled how he'd seen Granda Frank (whom he never knew) and how they'd walked hand in hand through a big open field and then both chased a single black bird, laughing all the while! Needless to say, I was overwhelmed. I pulled the car over and cried my heart out, their little voices asking what was wrong from the back seat. Nothing was wrong, but in that moment, I was connected again with my father.

I wonder, do we carry memories in our DNA and pass these on to our children, forever keeping our ancestors alive, echoes of the past inherited and passed on to us through dreams and feelings?

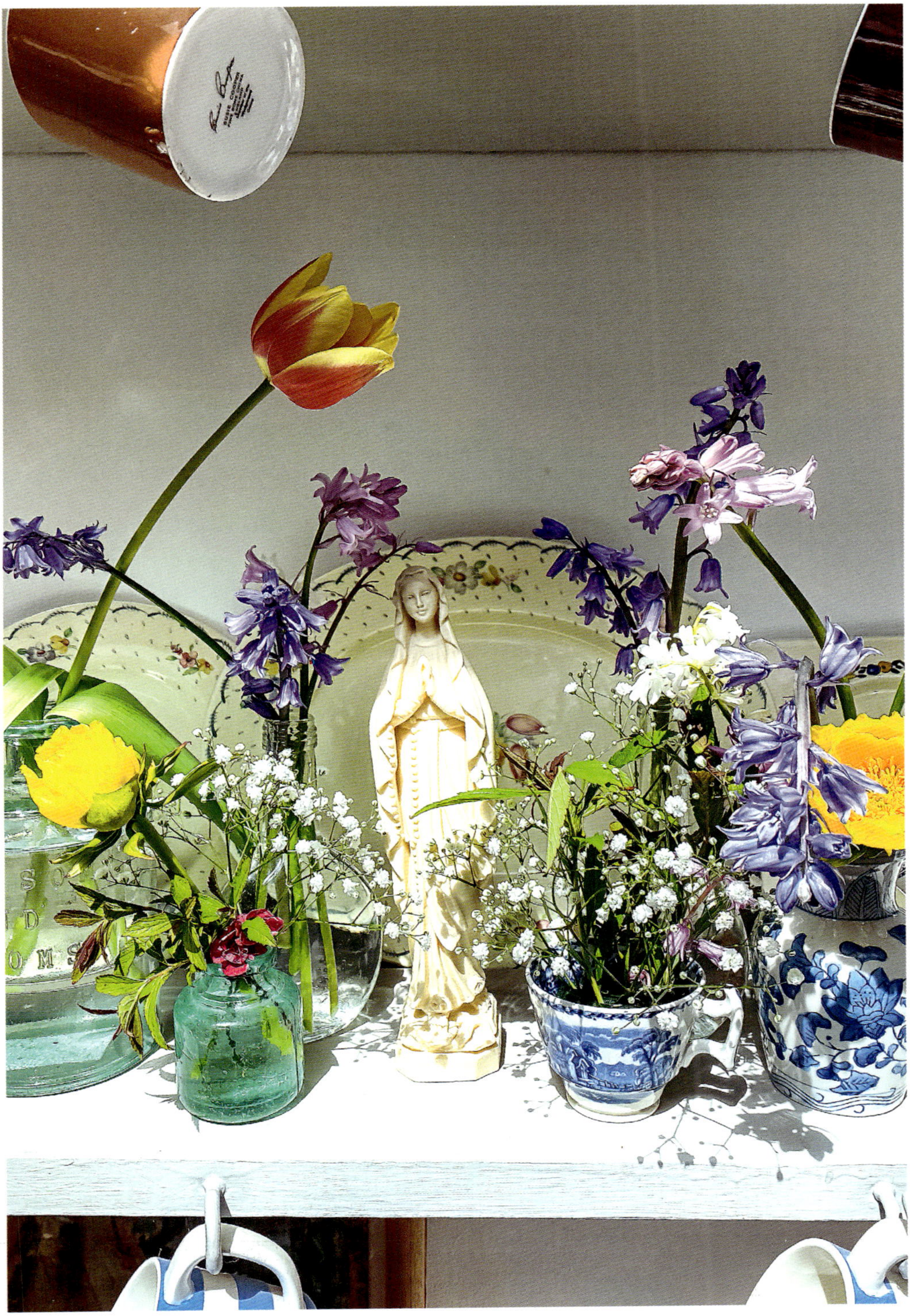

Mysteries

I found the blessed candle and I lit it for you.
Memories bring the light and I have neither peace nor calm
but a knowing.
A stillness hung in the air,
the flame flickered on, and I sat alone
and sent a prayer up for you again,
my breath still warm, but I knew.

The window's open and your soul flew.
I sat with the flickering flame
and sent a prayer up for you again,
for I knew, I knew.

A quiet man looked up,
the robin tilted its head and hopped.
I knew that I had lived
and you had lost this one thing precious to you.

You were precious but fool's gold,
Your hard edges fixed and set,
and I, your amber amulet.
The world waited for dawn,
and I slowly set upon a new life, a still life.

With this moment forever frozen in time
I sat, I sat and knew with all my knowing
that you were gone.
Time had told your story,
time had let go of you,
stopped the flow of you,
and I knew, I just knew.

So now this love I have for you is a time-waster's passion,
for you are gone
And I have all the time in the world to do anything.
Full Moon, New Moon, intentions set;
and what I have asked for would turn ears to the wind.

I found the candle and I lit it for you.
I sit alone and I think of you.
I'm coming home and I wish for you.
I wait for dawn and I dream of you.

―――

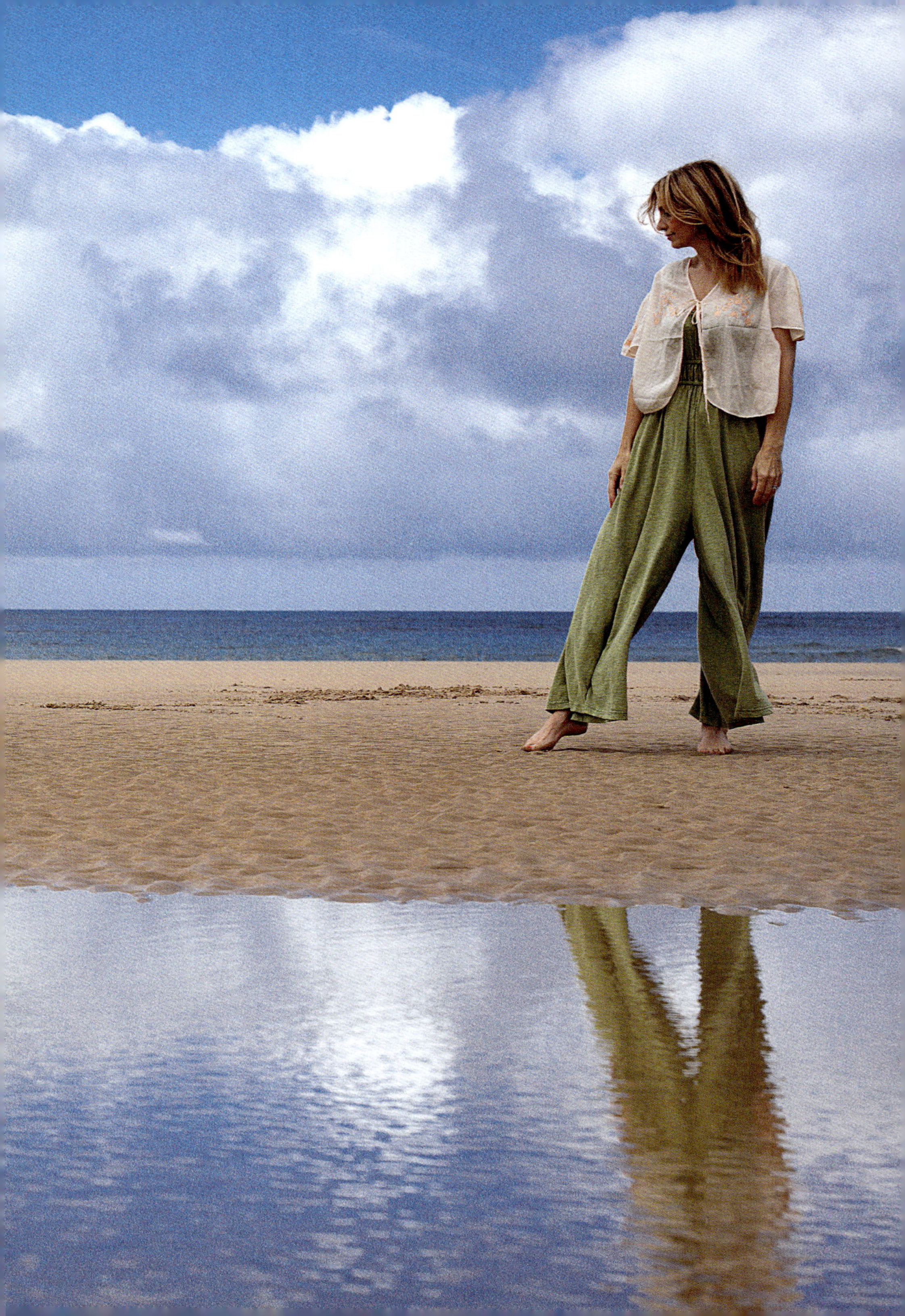

Inishowen

I was born on 21 July 1975 to Teresa Dillon, aged forty-four, and Frank Dillon, fifty-four – I know, I know – God love them! I'm the youngest of six, my eldest sister being twenty years to the month older than me and my nearest sibling, Francis, who is seven years older. To say I was a big surprise and a shock is an understatement. My father was a building contractor, he owned his own firm and had two ladies working for him in the office just off the side of our house. Meanwhile, my mother had given up running a busy café and clothes shop in Claudy to take care of the family. I'm sure she felt she was well past all the baby stuff … and then I appeared.

I absolutely loved the excitement and bustle of home. Growing up, I used to watch and wait for the convent bus to pull up outside the house, for I knew as soon as my brother and sisters got off it, that was when the *craic* began. In the quiet of our kitchen, I sat watching Mammy making pancakes on the griddle, ready to feed Francis and the girls who were arriving hungry from school. Now it was full on teenage time – stories, laughing, grumbling and plenty of sibling teasing as

On Five Finger Strand in Co. Donegal. One of my favourite beaches in Inishowen.

we all sat down to eat. Most evenings I would perch on a chair stacked high with cushions at the table as they did their homework, me pretending to do joined up writing, not wanting to miss out on anything, producing lines and lines of scribbles that made perfect sense to me.

Weekends were full of the girls' friends calling round, the upstairs bedrooms becoming a hothouse of teenage hormones, the latest eighties fashion, records spinning on the turntable, leg warmers, perms, rainbow eyeshadow and cigarette smoke curling out the window. They'd all be getting ready to go out and I was usually planted in amongst them all, transfixed, always watching and always listening. I knew – and I was well warned – that smoking was forbidden, so I often bribed them. "Let me try on your eyeshadow or else I'll get Daddy!"

I remember one evening when Mammy was out and Daddy was watching the news. I walked over to him and I told him I really needed his help to reach something down from upstairs. I took his arm and led him upstairs into the room where there were at least six girls smoking out the window. In a blind panic the butts were thrown out the window and just happened to land at the feet of my mother who was in the garden below – all hell broke loose. I was definitely a "wee bitch" at times and I knew it.

Saturday morning was always quiet, teens asleep, Mammy making a fry and Daddy having a well-earned lie-in. I was usually up with the birds and couldn't wait to get the house busy. I'd wait impatiently until I'd hear Mammy say to me, usually late in the morning, "It's time they were up now," and I'd eagerly take my tin whistle and blow it as hard as I could in their bedrooms to get them all up. They really hated that. I've always loved it when we we're together and I think that's why I still love family get-togethers now. Since I'm the only one to have moved away from home I enjoy the power I have, the ability to gather us all around Mammy's kitchen table for a drink when I'm back home, and it fills my heart with the same happiness I felt as a wean. For the 'wean' is pretty much the only name I was ever known by, as my parents' friends, aunties, and uncles would come to visit and exclaim, "Sure, that's not the wean, is it?" or, "Where is the wean?" like I was some wee mystery or an alien of sorts and they'd study me to see who I was like.

When you're the wean, you know how to act the wean. I'd be instructed by one of the older ones to ask Daddy if we could go out for dinner, or to give someone a fiver for the cinema, or to drive to Coleraine to shop. "If Cara asks him, he'll do it!" they'd say. In fact, this happened right up to the end when he passed in 2003, I was always the wee pet and struggle to remember a time he said no to me.

I suppose this gives a little insight into my early home life, but then there were the holidays, all of us piled into the car, trailer attached, heading to Donegal at every chance we had. We were sitting on squashed pillows, duvets, sheets, surrounded by everything but the kitchen sink, and I'm certain it wasn't much of a holiday or a break for my poor mother.

My daddy's whole attire would change from dark work clothes – so often covered in brick dust and splinters – to light, white trousers, short-sleeved shirts without a tie, and sports jackets. The lightness of his appearance, I believe, reflected the lightness in his heart.

My father had built a house near Greencastle on the Inishowen peninsula sometime in the early seventies and we would go there at Easter, bank holiday weekends, and for

Greencastle Harbour at dusk, looking beautiful.

the whole of the summer holidays. The house was regularly filled to the brim with friends and family all summer long. There were late nights spent in Kealy's Bar & Restaurant just across the road from Greencastle harbour, and I would drink football specials with the foam on top, pretending it was red Guinness, and then take myself for wee wanders around the harbour on my own or with my best friend Emma, while my parents and their friends laughed all the day long, together with Gertie and Willie Kealy behind the bar. (Kealy's restaurant would, years later, go on to become a trendy spot where celebrities and politicians would be spotted enjoying delicious seafood chowder.)

My mother and Gertie would often sit back and laugh at the great success Gertie's son, James, had made of the place. Looking back now, these days were very special, they were almost sacred for me. As the teenagers gradually stopped coming on holidays with my parents (for they had better things to be at) I suddenly had both my parents all to myself. We would drive the length and breadth of Donegal, stopping at beaches and restaurants, at sessions in Ardara and discovering new vistas, all the while listening to Mary Black singing "Hard Times" on the car stereo. My daddy would exclaim, "What in the name of God could that woman know about hard times?!" Me and Mammy would roll our eyes and turn it up even louder.

We'd explore the stone walls of Bloody Foreland in rain and sunshine, always pulling into a pub for my parents to enjoy a drink. Somehow, they always ended up chatting to people who knew someone they knew.

I got my first tin whistle in Donegal Town and became

Our children, Colm, Noah and Elizabeth with their cousin Aoibheann and friend, Ellen enjoying playing in a session in Moville.

obsessed with Planxty and the Bothy Band. I played the whistle along to the music in the back of the car, I was sad to put it down when we had to get out and appreciate a view ... but what a view it was. The hairs would stand up on the back of my neck, listening to Dolores Keane sing on the car stereo, or to Mary Black's rendition of "A Song for Ireland" on my Walkman as I watched the sun set from the top of a cliff. My parents, the music, and that Irish landscape were all that mattered to me.

Myself and my mother walked miles upon miles of white, sandy Donegal beaches, year after year, gathering driftwood for her to take home to the garden, quiet and happy in each other's company. My daddy even taught me to drive on the beach in Bunbeg one quiet summer's evening when no one

Noah, throwing stones into the surf on Pollan Strand, Inishowen.

else was about – I was twelve years old. He eventually gave in to my whingeing, after I insisted that I was fit for it … and off I took. I trusted him and he trusted me.

The happiness in me seemed to mirror the happiness in my parents, and even at an early age I noticed that it began the very minute we were past the checkpoint on the border from Derry to Donegal, crossing from the North to the South. Even as I write this now I am beginning to get a knot in my stomach, that familiar feeling of anxiety – as a child, it was often at its worst on the approach to these border crossings. As a wee girl, my eye-level view out of the rear window of the car was of a soldier's waistband, fingers wrapped dangerously around a machine gun, and barbed wire … endless barbed wire. I rarely saw the soldiers' faces, only from the chest down, just their camouflaged trousers and big heavy-looking boots, and the sound of strange accents shouting, "Pull over, step out of the vehicle!" and then my father muttering "Bastards" under his breath. For we were going on our holiday and there was rarely a time we could just go freely, without hindrance.

Sometimes, if we were lucky, it was relatively quick, just a few walkie talkies and signals, maybe just a quick look at the driver's licence and then, "Okay, Mr Dillon, have a good time". However, it was more often, "Okay, out you all get – open the boot," then searches, enquiries, "Where did you come from today? Where are you going? How long? Why?" This was followed by yet more waiting, more boots stomping around the car, guns always pointed, more walkie talkies. The radio was turned off, the English accents saying, "Come on mate," but my father was no "mate" of theirs.

I grew to hate that word, 'mate'. It was only used by

British soldiers, used when they were making me hold my breath, when there was no music in the car, and when I was scared that they would take my daddy, that he'd never be allowed back to us. Then, with the border checkpoint behind us, the escape and the freedom would come, and it was incredible. Windows rolled down, the radio turned on again, and the yellow – yellow everywhere. Yellow in my mind and in my tummy, yellow lines on the road and yellow gorse that lined the roads and led us all the way to Greencastle, and yellow Golden Crisp chocolate bars you could only buy across the border in the Free State, and the yellow of Chicken Maryland banana and pineapple fritters that we would eat in McNamara's Hotel in Moville, and the yellow Tayto crisps that I'd munch, sitting up high on a barstool with my daddy sipping a Guinness by my side. Sure – it's no wonder at all that yellow is my favourite colour.

Now, I must stress that this is *my* story. Throughout the seventies and eighties I didn't experience any great personal suffering as a result of The Troubles. My parents, aunts, and uncles, on the other hand, experienced more than their fair share of heartache, danger and endless worry during those troubled years in County Derry. But those are *their* stories, not mine – and although their experiences have been hugely important throughout the landscape of my youth, they haven't defined my world view; in fact, quite the contrary. I was lucky to have been brought up within a loving family and feel I was somehow sheltered from the worst of it. They'd lived through Bloody Sunday, internment, the shootings, the beatings, and had shown over and over again that resilience and true community spirit could pave the way for a better future.

I was a part of that future, and even at the age of five, when I was brought along as the town gathered to pray for the local hunger striker, Kevin Lynch, I was aware of the closeness and the power of the community.

However, I'll always remember the sad feeling I'd get when returning from our summers across the border in Inishowen, coming back through the border checkpoints in the rain and eventually driving up Dungiven main street, past the imposing police barracks (for a while Dungiven's best-known landmark). There was the look-out tower, complete with army guns pointing out, and me wondering if I was guilty for having enjoyed myself away from it all. For this was our home and this was our normal – our day-to-day reality. Back in the house the family were all reunited. The *craic* was ninety, and there was so much gossip to catch up on, but there was also danger on the radio droning relentlessly in the background, reminding us of new bomb scares and shootings, more "trouble" – there was always so much news. As we went back to school in September, the reality was at times quite grim: soldiers in our garden, soldiers hiding in the bushes on the way to school, armoured Land Rovers patrolling the streets of our town…

My childhood best friend, Emma, and I dressed as "Bridge Over Troubled Waters" for a parade in the town.

I remember the first time I went to England as a teenager to perform a gig with my band, Óige, and we watched the evening news in a hotel room. I thought it was strange, but there was no mention of bombs and shootings – no footage of armoured vehicles,

Coming Home

of barbed wire, nor sight nor sound of balaclavas and guns. For a split second I almost thought The Troubles had ended … and then I came home and realised we had a very different type of news, a different kind of trouble that didn't seem to make it across the water. But God, it made me love where I'm from with an even greater passion; the people there, what my parents had lived with, what the community had suffered, and my pride for my town and its people grew stronger and stronger.

The GAA club just down the road from my home in Dungiven, not only matches, but ceilidhs, concerts and celebrations all happen here.

Inishowen

Hold the thought for a moment,
Let there be peace to let the spirit remember.
The way the river winds,
The smell of sunshine melting tar;
Yellow lines on the road
Leading the way to Inishowen.

Leaving behind the tangle of barbed wire
For a tangle of yellow gorse.
Leaving behind the radio, now paused.
Instead there's music, no cause,
Singing 'Hard Times Come Again No More".

Leaving behind solid thumping boots and camouflaged thoughts,
Car boots opening and closing,
Searching, and stopping the flow of everything.
Now freedom is barefoot on the sand.

Leaving behind prayers for the suffering.
Instead, prayers of thanksgiving for the land.
Everything's yellow and I'm happy cause you're happy.

Coastal paths and glassy water,
Driftwood smoothed by Lough Swilly's chatter.
Seaweed tangled in our toes,
Swimming off the Atlantic coast in rain and sunshine,
For God knows we knew freedom when it came.
And release from the radio; booming noise,
That background noise, forever in our ears.

So you'd find us here,
Lying on russet rocks,
hiding amongst orange and green
Montbretia blooms.
Unnoticed,
Unseen,
Chameleons of the North.

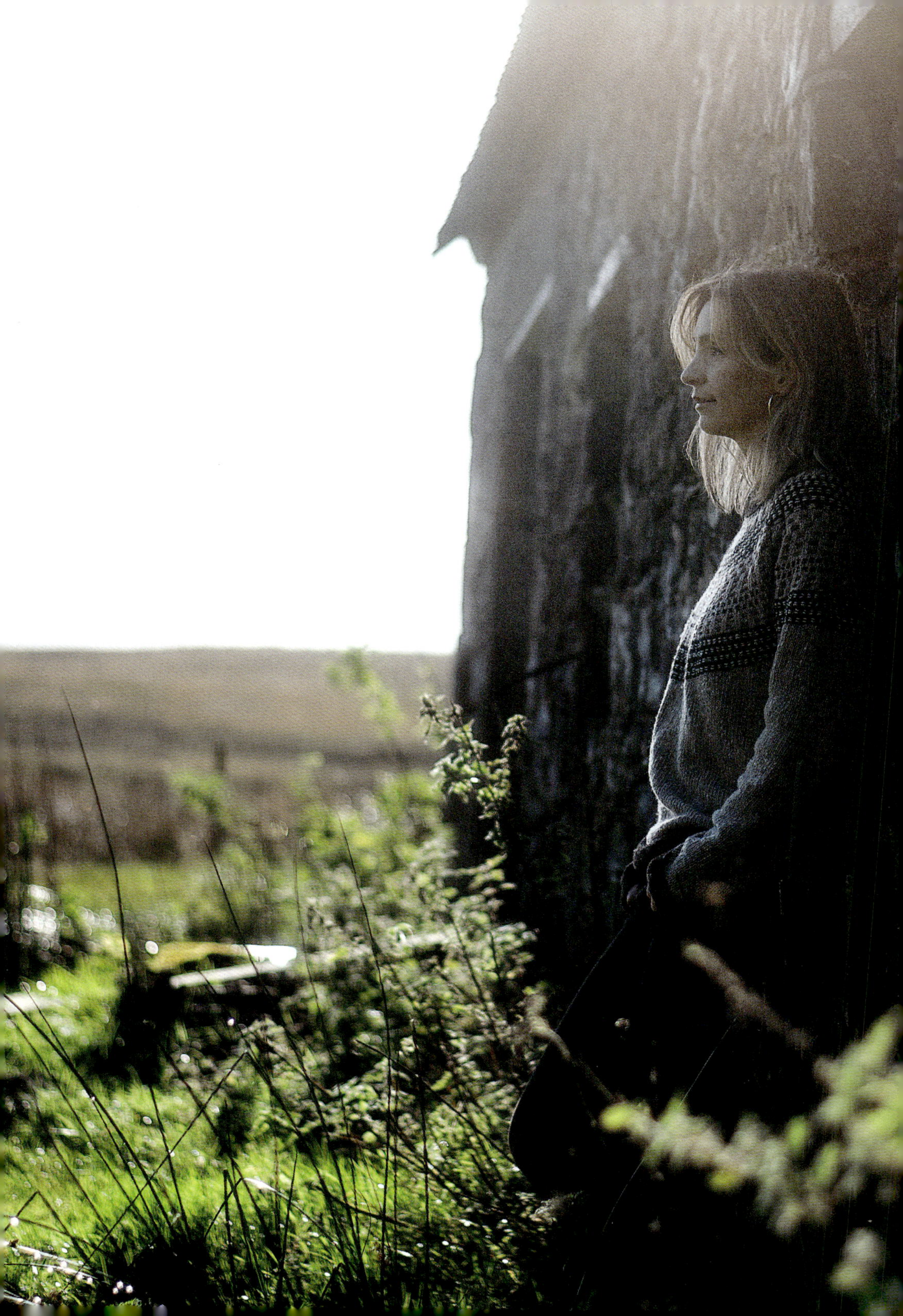

Clear the Path

On a shelf in my house, I have photographs of the grandparents that I never knew. I've always enjoyed studying old pictures of my relatives, searching their faces to see if there are resemblances in me and my children. It's their eyes – always their eyes – that seem to speak to me. I want to know more about them, what they did, how they lived, for we are part of an ever-evolving story.

Because my mother is in her nineties now, when I hear her speak of her younger days, I realise what a privilege it is to be so connected to a such a completely different time in history. She is a genuine treasure trove of wisdom and, like many older people who have witnessed such incredible change, possesses a far deeper understanding of what life is really about and the things that truly matter.

Nowadays, we are so connected to the wider world. We have so much information to hand and yet, I often feel we

At the door of Eslin.

may have forgotten to stop and remember who we are. Are we strangers to ourselves? Do we really know ourselves at all? For me, those belonging to us who've gone before are the key. I'm so fortunate to have been brought up in a place where traditional music and song is celebrated and held in the utmost importance. It means I've had a head start in getting to grips with people and places from the past through the haunting melodies they wrote, and the songs that shine a light on the emotions and stories of the people. Of course, I know how important the oral tradition is, but it's particularly so in my wee corner of the world. The wealth of stories, songs, myths and melodies from Dungiven and the surrounding area is extraordinary and a huge part of how we keep our ancestors alive.

The idea for the poem "Clear The Path" came to me when I was literally weeding our garden path. I had time and space to think, my mind being free while my hands were busy. It was during the pandemic and I was thinking *"What is life all about?"* I was feeling an overwhelming desire to see my family, and yet I realised I was connected to them in a place in my mind beyond time and space. And so this must stand true when we go back beyond the timeline we live in now. I want to keep this path clear for my own ancestors to speak to me. I want to make sure that this path doesn't become overgrown or littered with weeds.

We see different family traits in our children, like they're keeping the past alive in front of our very eyes. There's a saying where I'm from: *"You didn't take it*

My father's parents, Frank and Elizabeth Dillon.

off the ditch." I've been asked "Where did you get your singing voice from? Did you have lessons? Did you practice a lot?" The answer, maybe surprisingly, is no. My voice is just there in me and around me and now probably the biggest part of what makes me. My mother talks of *her* mother singing beautifully by the fireside; singing and sewing by the light of a Tilley lamp. She remembers as a child, her father and mother going out on their *ceilidh* and coming home, up the lane at night, singing away to their heart's content. I wonder who else went before her in the long line of ancestry? Who else sang a song that filled their hearts with joy? Or perhaps entertained others with their voice? Or simply lulled a baby to sleep?

Singing for me transcends time and space. When I sing, I'm receiving the greatest gift of all. It's like a sacred space, a circle around me. I feel a deep connection between myself and the audience.

When I stand on the land my parents came from, I cannot describe the feeling I get, it's almost addictive, like a hunger that demands feeding ... I need to know more. I imagine the voices working on the land, calling to each other, singing with each other. I can almost hear a fiddle playing and the laughter of a good night's *craic* in that old house and I also feel the sadness and heartache that that space holds for those who were left behind when family emigrated, those who had to leave and were not able to return; a one-way ticket to an ever-hopeful future; the countless letters home and that sense of loss from both sides. I want to sing for them, or at least keep their memory alive, to tell their stories – my own oral tradition.

The Leaving Song

Hold out your hand, love,
We'll figure this out.
You don't need to leave and never look back.

You take your own time, love,
But give it a chance.
There's life in these fields like there's rhythm in dance.

Stay by my side, love,
And give up your doubt.
Your brother has gone and my time's running out.

The dew's on the grass,
We've finished the glass,
The dawn's on its way, love,
But my son leaves today.

They whisper your name, son,
Like they've put you to rest.
They've kissed you and blessed you we've all done our best.

And once I could swear, love,
I heard the wind sing.
It warned of this day and the cold it would bring.

These Northern lights shine, love,
Reflect on the Foyle
They'll light your way back to your own native soil.

The dew's on the grass,
We've finished the glass,
The dawn's on its way now,
But my son leaves today.
My son leaves today, Lord,
God help me I pray,
God help me I pray.

Slip out the door, love,
But don't say goodbye.
Just take one last look at this Northwestern sky.

―――

Written by Cara Dillon & Sam Lakeman.

Taken from the album *Wanderer*, released 2017

I wrote this song inspired by the stories Mammy told me when I was growing up about a tradition called the 'living wake'. When someone was emigrating (usually to America) they would organise a gathering of the family and community to celebrate the life of the one who was leaving, often on the night before they were due to leave. It was a chance to give them a great send-off, with everyone staying up all night dancing, singing and telling stories.

"The Leaving Song" is about a mother begging her son to stay, to not leave, for this is where he belongs. I wanted to try and express that sense of time running out, like the last hour of darkness, just before the first light of the morning brought with it the harsh reality of the situation and the heartache for all involved.

Mammy remembers gatherings in their house in Eslin when she was a small child, sometime in the 1930s. She says a fiddle always hung on the wall and one of the local men played it. There'd be dancing and she remembers sitting on the floor as a little girl while men danced with hobnail boots, sparks rising off the floor as they flew around the room. I've heard tales of houses falling silent in the early hours of the morning when all present realised the person who was leaving had already slipped away out the back door like a shadow into the night sky, all to avoid saying that difficult final goodbye.

Then came the sadness, the heartbreak, the pain of the loss. The atmosphere would change dramatically and the older women gathered together, lamenting, crying and singing, a tradition known as keening … a sound that would chill you to your very bones.

The thing I love about all of this is that sense of belonging to a community, the way people gathered around each other in times of need. I witnessed this firsthand at my own father's wake. Three days where the family were comforted, supported, and stories were told about him in his life by the hundreds of people who came from far and wide and shared in our grief.

Inside The Bing.

Clear The Path

Clear the path now,
Weeds have gathered on our ancestral trail.
Singers of songs long gone,
Poets, storytellers, artists, weavers,
Give in now and surrender to them.
Those from whom you came,
The long lines coursing through your veins.
Come on and fan the flames and concentrate,
For it's written on your son's face,
That light, shining through,
Blazing, in a moment of grace.

We are the daughters of women that we will become,
The trailblazers whose lives will never be done.
For they stood on this self-same soil,
Buried the seeds that germinated, birthed and fed
A new generation of tiny intricacies,
Forgotten family traits and oft-remembered eyes,
And hidden talents that reveal themselves
At the strangest of times.

Speak of them,
Search for them,
For they are true.

Speak of them,
Search for them,
For they hold you.

We are the daughters of women that we will become,
Whose lives can never be done.
Clear the path, clear the path.

My grandmother, Mary Mullan ... fit for it all.

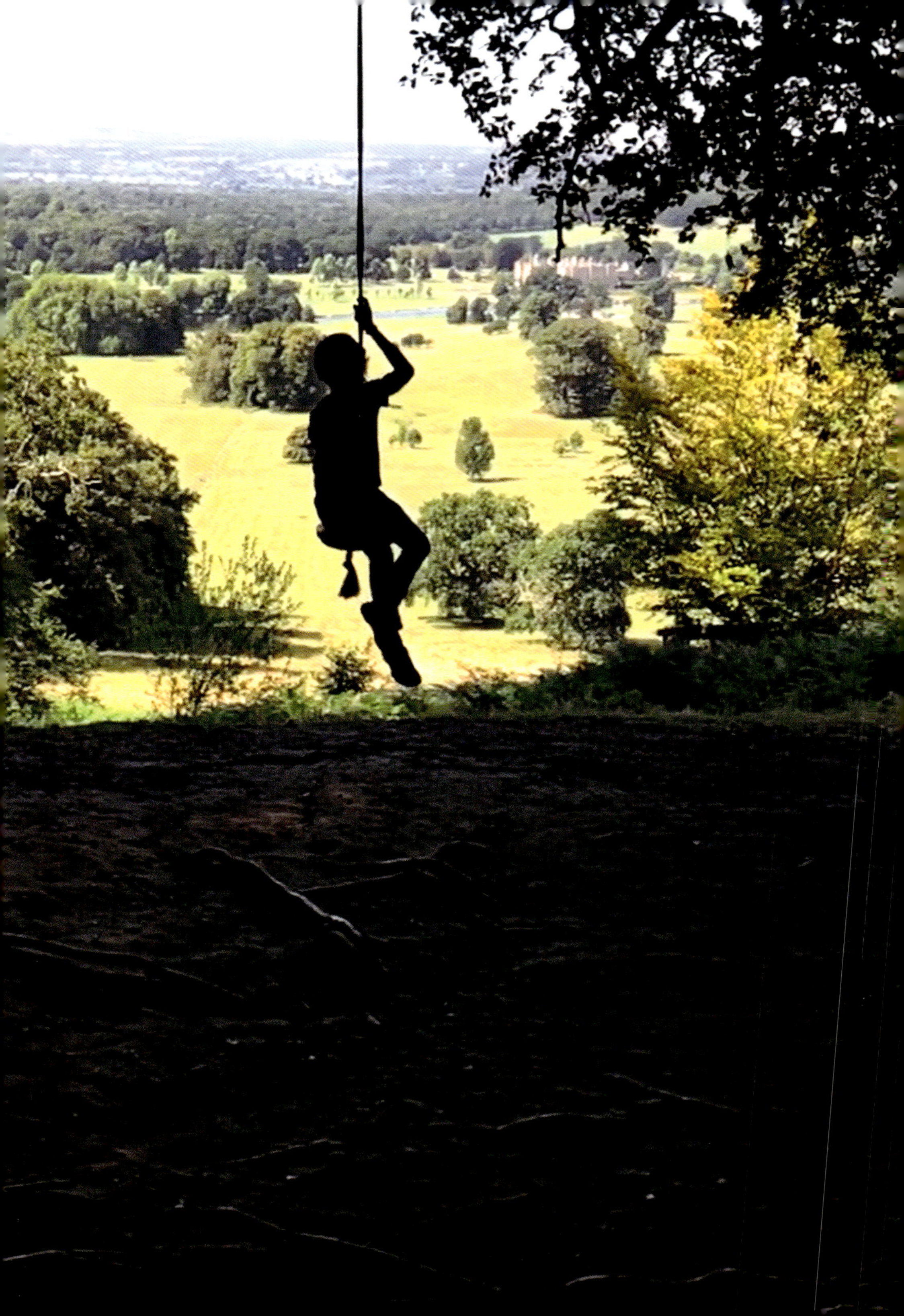

Giving

"Give anything, but give."

TERESA DILLON

When I close my eyes, I can see my mother rushing about, drawers opening and closing, the snap of a purse, the rustle of a paper bag, all of this happening the minute a visitor looked about to rise off their chair to head home. "Wait a minute…" she'd say, and she'd be up and out to the kitchen to see what she could give them. If they had weans, it would be a few coins, but normally a loaf of freshly made wheaten bread, soda scones or something else that she may have bought months before and threw on top of her wardrobe, knowing someone would like it. "Take it with ye now!" However, if anyone tried to give her something in return, she'd scowl. "Sure, you'll take all the good out of it now if you start that business!" You could say she's generous to a fault.

When she arrived to Dungiven from Glenullin as a newly married woman of twenty-two, people soon figured out that

Colm, enjoying the view from "Heaven's Gate" in Somerset. Still one of our favourite walks.

my mother had a big heart. Shortly after moving, she was called for to wash and prepare the corpse of an old lady whom she'd begun visiting regularly. Someone had arrived at her door in a fluster saying, "My granny asked for Mrs. Dillon to come to sort things out". Mammy says it was seen as a great honour and privilege to be asked, and so, probably with a lot of hesitation but no questions asked, she just got on with it. "I'd never done anything like that before," she said.

"I'm not bloody surprised!" I said back to her. I'm definitely sure that I wouldn't have been so willing.

Then there was the time the local parish priest asked her to visit an old lady who lived alone on the mountain. She was poor and wasn't doing so well. So my dear mother made the journey, arriving at her house to find it not only in an awful state, but also filled with cats – cats absolutely everywhere, in the kitchen, bathroom, sitting room and bedroom, and the smell was truly shocking. Well, she got the old woman "sorted out" *(God only knows what that meant)* and the house cleaned up, only to end up catching a horrific dose of something very serious indeed and ending up in quarantine in Altnagelvin Hospital for a few weeks. She was not very well at all, her bed cautiously placed behind plastic curtains with the doctors asking her where on earth she had been, for they had never come across a disease quite like that before in Derry.

"Give anything, but don't die trying!"

CARA DILLON

And so, as the saying goes, "*As the old cock crows the young cock learns*". I believe all six of us, in watching the comings and goings of our mother, have developed our own quirky and unique ways of giving. And me? Well, I definitely get it wrong sometimes – but I try, I really, really do.

When my nephew, Odhrán, moved to Somerset and ended up living just a stone's throw down the road from me, I couldn't get over it. I was so excited at the prospect of looking after him, of having a family member from home on my doorstep. I'd do what I knew 'the auntie' was expected to do and absolutely nothing was going to get in my way. He was a twenty-eight-year-old, independent young man, but that didn't matter one iota to me. I would regularly have a wee dish on his doorstep waiting for him when he came home from work, or some of those soda scones that I talk of – and boy, was I proud of myself. He would laugh and ask me what I was up to next, threatening to tell my sisters that I wasn't looking after him well enough.

Then one evening while he was in my house, it all came to a head. I'd insisted he take the leftovers home from the dinner and he said I needed to "get a grip", and that he wasn't "back in Dungiven now", that he actually loved cooking for himself, and I should just go ahead and eat my own bloody leftovers! (All just a bit of *craic* I might add).

But as you can imagine, that didn't stop me. I continued in other ways: I gave him things I thought he might need, like a coffee table, some of my old curtains, an old fridge magnet. I dreamt up countless reasons to invite him over just so I could cook for him, proving to no one but myself that I was looking after him – whether he wanted it or not. I mean – God help my own weans when they leave home!

A few years ago, our very close friends went through an incredibly difficult time. She had been diagnosed with cancer and was in pieces. During a horrendous day when she had been rushed to hospital in an ambulance, her husband arrived at our house later the same night, a truly broken man. We were all beside ourselves with worry.

As he left our house that night, my instinct kicked in and I asked him if he'd like me to make him a pot of soup, to which he replied, "No. I suppose I can call in tomorrow if I want a bowl," to which I responded, "Well then, what about a casserole?"

He looked at me square in the eyes. The man was bereft, exhausted … and he looked at me like I had horns on my head. "No, I'm all right, Cara. I'll call in if I'm hungry".

Well, the next morning, I was on the phone to my mother, filling her in on all the dramatic news, when I got around to telling her about him refusing my soup. "You what?" she barked. "Cara, you don't ask, you just give! What in the name of God have I reared?" Well, lessons were learned and I will never ask again in my life.

Not many things can equal the feeling when you give from the heart. I have to say, Sam is particularly good at this. I've received some of the most beautiful and thoughtful gifts from him over the years. He has a remarkable knack for turning up with just the right thing that will put a huge smile on my face, whether it's from a beautiful shop or a skip. What I love most is that it doesn't need to be for any particular occasion. It's just knowing that I'm in his thoughts, that's the thing that really counts.

When our children were small, we would take them for long walks through the beautiful forests here in Somerset, and I'd be presented with lots of little, precious gifts – sticks, pine cones wrapped in leaves, smooth stones, feathers and tiny pieces of coloured glass. I have kept a few of these things because I can't bring myself to get rid of them, for they bring

Colm and Noah.

A young Elizabeth in a sunbeam in the forest near our home in Somerset.

me straight back to the days of cold, red noses and tiny fingers wrapped around my hand with happiness in abundance. One of my boys learned to whittle wood using a little pocketknife we bought him for his birthday. For a while he sat happily at the back of our garden and made lots of treasures. I used to look out and see him perched on a log, content amongst the bushes, whittling away.

On the day before my birthday last year, I clocked one of our sons in town. He told me he was on a mission to buy me a birthday present. Later that night, I heard him tell his brother that he'd got me a great present and was sure I would absolutely love it.

Before bedtime that night, I heard a scratching, scraping noise coming from the top of the house. I thought we had a mouse. When I went up to investigate, I heard a squeal: "Stop! Go away!"

My other son was very busy making my birthday gift. He'd panicked that he hadn't gone to buy me one earlier and, after learning his brother wouldn't share the one he'd bought, he'd gone out into the garden, grabbed a stick, and was whittling away at it like his life depended on it.

The next morning, I was presented with the gifts, one of them a whittled mushroom-shaped object presented to me in the manner a happy dog presents its owner with a stick. I can't tell you how much I love it. The other was a beautiful hand-thrown, painted mug that I now drink my tea from. I look at the mushroom-type stick on the shelf and it warms the cockles of my heart. Both of these gifts are loved in equal measure.

One of the precious home-made gifts given to me by one of our boys.

"The meaning of life is to find your gift.

The purpose of life is to give it away"

PABLO PICASSO

Giving

I would not go empty-handed
For it's been drummed into me,
Give anything, but give.

A hand-tied bunch from the garden,
A stone smoothed by the love of a hand,
Sea glass of blue and green,
Sharp edges gone now by the shape-shifting sands.
Give anything, but give.

Feathers found in the forest,
A cross made of rushes,
A stick, weathered, not broken,
Give anything, but give.

A penny from your pocket,
Hair for the locket,
A book, dog-eared and tired,
That might just hold a mystery unfolded.

In my pocket I found from you
The sweetest treasures wrapped in leaves.
We followed the trail into the light
And searched the forest far and wide.

And all the while, side by side,
Gathering our scattered thoughts.
You have my heart, what will I do?
For now we're coming home.

In my pocket, I found from you
A handful of our memories.
We followed the trail into the night
And left the forest far behind.

You have my heart, what will I do?
For now we're coming home.

———

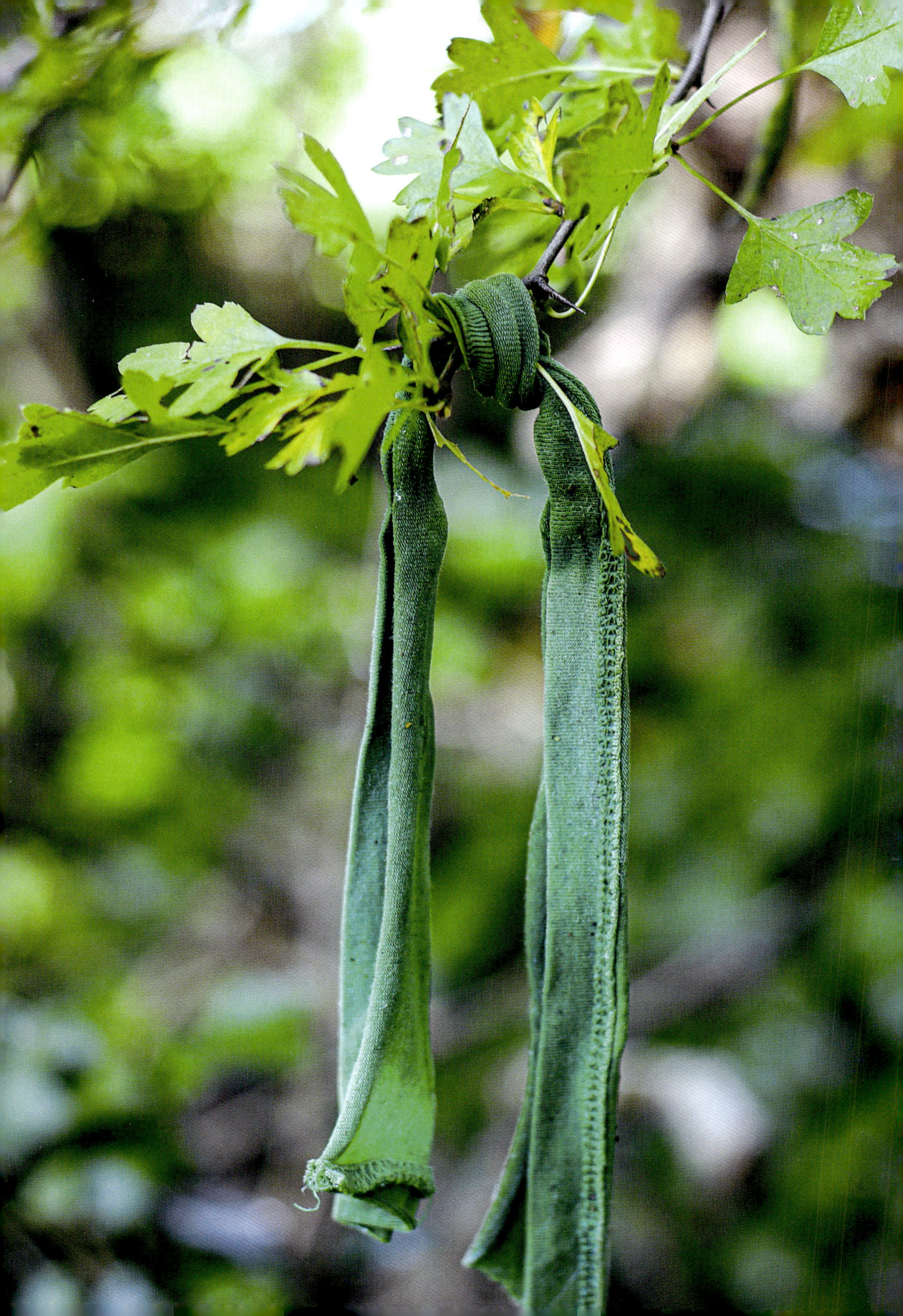

The Cure

"It's far from your arse, and you don't have to sit on it!" Mammy would recite this anytime we complained of an ache or pain, and we'd be expected to just run on – unless of course you did have to sit on it!

The talk of cures was very common when I was growing up. Not only did I hear my mother talking about the various plants and their healing properties that grew around the hedgerows of her home in Glenullin, but also my father was a sucker for taking anything given to him, or for visiting a healer if he thought it would help him. In fact, many folk I know would be prepared to try anything if they felt they'd benefit in one way or another from it. There is a great power in mind over matter, and believing in something beyond our understanding, which I find both fascinating and beautiful.

My mother swore on the power of nettle soup to cleanse the blood. It was an annual spring-clean for the body which, alongside her and her siblings eating the berries that grew in the ditches on their way home from school,

A clootie tied to a branch above the Well near the old priory in Dungiven.

My uncle, George Mullan. The best man in the Glen.

probably gave their immune system a healthy boost each year. She and my auntie Margaret talk of eating sullocks, sloe berries, blackcurrants and redcurrants. Every summer, their mother would find a plant called bogbine which had a little flower shaped like a pink and white star, raised just above the bog water. She would boil up the roots and they would drink the water every morning – it was said to be excellent for the blood, another spring tonic, although she said it tasted absolutely foul. I've since discovered that all over the North of Ireland people claimed this was a cure for colds and congestion, arthritis, skin issues, indigestion and constipation. Could this be where one of Mammy's other favourite sayings comes from: *"A cure for coughs and colds and sore arseholes and pimples on the diddy."* For it seems to be a cure for everything.

My uncle George has worked this land his whole life, the very same land where he and his siblings grew up. He is one of the kindest men you could ever hope to meet, still a bachelor in his eighties and devoted to his extraordinary sheepdogs.

When Sam and I got married, he landed at my mammy's house on the day before the wedding with a gift for us. He pushed a large wedge of cash into my hand saying, "Ah sure, Cara, I only had to go and sell a couple of sheep for ye!"

The closeness between George and his sisters is very strong, and although they're all getting very old, they still have a weekly ritual of visiting him in his wee cottage out in the glen, where they gather in his kitchen for tea and to share the news. Up until very recently, my mother and my aunties would bring a number of empty bottles for the weekly visit, filling them with the fresh spring water that

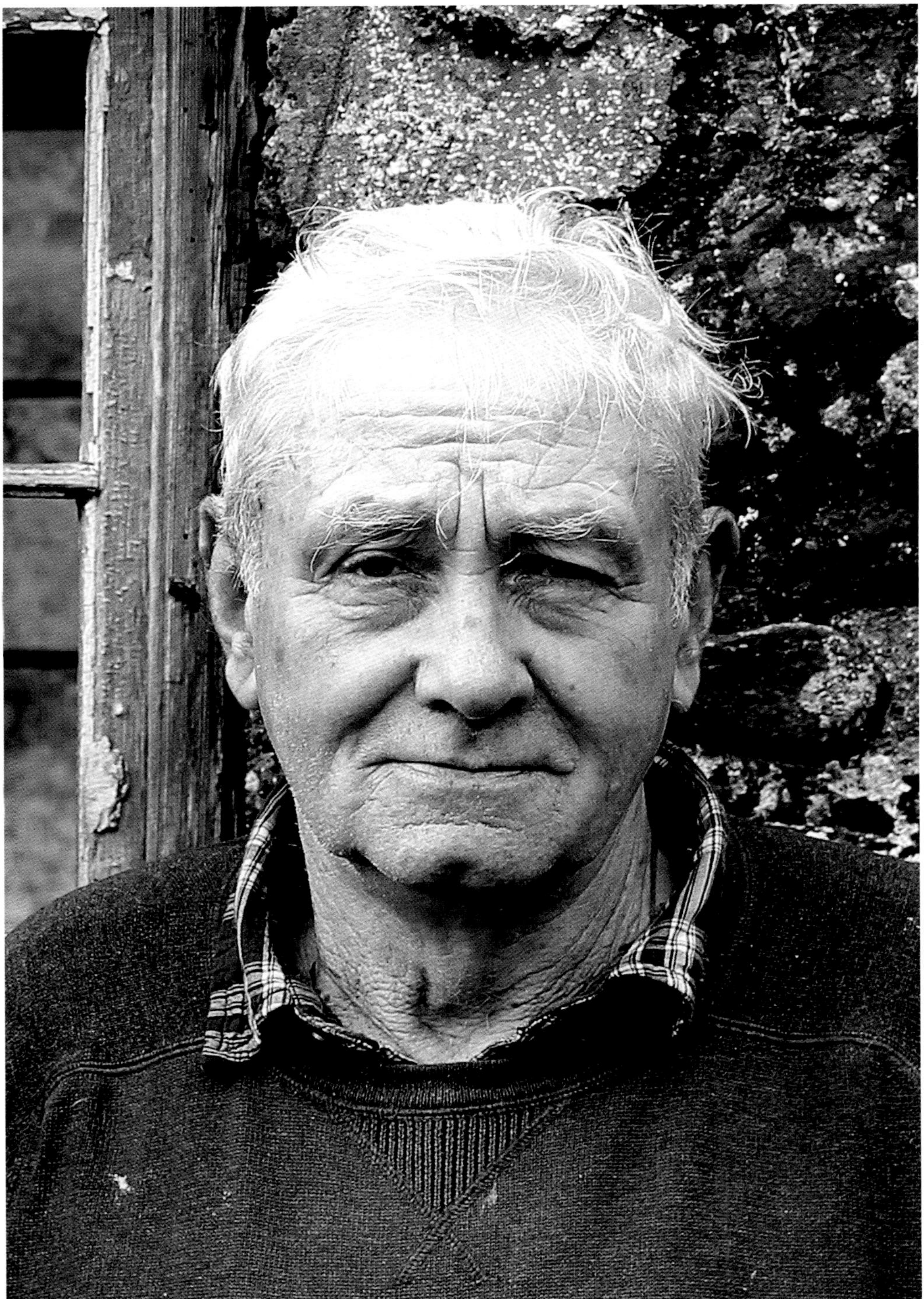

came bubbling up to his outside tap. They would rather drink this unfiltered mountain stream water than the sanitised offerings from the town supply. Litres of this spring water filled our fridge and not many of us got to drink it because my father swore it was a great cure for everything, drinking gallons of the stuff.

Although he tried manys the remedy over the years, which kept us all in entertainment, it wasn't all about this pure mountain dew. My father had a contact just over the border in Donegal for poitín*. It would arrive every now and then in a clear, unmarked bottle and – wait for it – wasn't even for him to drink, but to rub on all his aching joints. I swear that if he'd lit a match he'd have gone up in a puff of smoke … but it didn't end there.

Healers could be found in and around the area who carried the cure for all sorts of ailments. One particular occasion comes to mind when one of my sisters (I can't say which) headed off to see a man over in Cookstown who had the cure for haemorrhoids. They said a prayer together and she was duly sent home with two horse chestnuts to hold, being given strict instructions to keep them safe and dry. Apparently, in three days she was completely sorted.

In Dungiven town, we have the wonderful Lucy Vickie whom I've known my whole life. We used to go to *fleadhs* together with her daughter, Maranna, who's a fine traditional singer. Lucy has the cure for whooping cough, receiving this power as a result of marrying a man with the same surname. She told me there would never be money exchanged when curing someone and that's how you'd know it was the real deal.

Lucy's father was also well known for miles around for having the cure for asthma, which was handed down from generation to generation, to the seventh son of a seventh son. She told me that she takes off her wedding ring, makes the sign of a cross and rubs the ring on the child's eyes two or three times before telling them, "We'll pray to Our Lady for a week after." She also said, "As a healer, you must always give them something to take away with them, that's the deal. Sometimes, when it's a child, it's just a lump of sugar."

When you pass by Dungiven along the new road from Derry to Belfast, you might glimpse an ancient standing stone in a field near St Patrick's Chapel. On the opposite side of this road, a short distance away, you'll find the old twelfth-century Augustinian priory which houses the tomb of the great O'Cahan Chief, Cooey na Gall. As a child I would go to this ancient place on nature walks. I'd do grave rubbings and we'd have picnics and play hide and seek. I've always felt a peaceful energy there. In fact, in one of my most popular songs I pay homage to the O'Cahan clan, the old priory and Benbradagh, which is the name of the mountain which stands proudly watching over Dungiven town. Its name translates as "the hill of the thieves."

---

* pronounced "Potcheen". Irish moonshine.

The Hill of Thieves

(song)

For too long time I've been a stranger here,
To the hills above Glenshane,
And your rocks and your rain,
Where the silent souls haunt the priory walls,
In the wind they sing "Come away, come away."

To the murmuring stream with the town below
And the babbling swell of winding Roe,
And you still might hear the great O'Cahan Clan,
"Come away," they say, "to The Benedy Glen."

Where the Hound of the Plain has walked this land
And the loneliest mile, with a sword in his hand,
And his blood runs still, in every stream and glen,
And his home can be seen from the Hill of the Thieves.

For too long time I've been a stranger here,
To the hills above Glenshane,
And your rocks and your rain,
Where the silent souls haunt the priory walls,
In the wind they sing, "Come away, come away,
Come away."

———

Written by Cara Dillon & Sam Lakeman.
Appears on Cara's album, *Hill of Thieves*, released 2009

Nestled beside the priory and hidden among a tangle of ferns and hawthorn branches is a holy well. The well is actually a large pre-Christian bullaun* stone which fills with rainwater and is said to cure warts and other skin conditions. Friends, family and my own children have all visited this well over the years. We bring a rag or cloth (clootie), dip it in the water and rub it on our skin, leaving it behind, tied to branch above. As the cloth rots, your skin condition goes with it.

Throughout history, woman traditionally protected wells such as this one and the mythical water contained within. I've become fascinated with the important role they played in healing and protecting the land and its people; but for now, this female 'guardian of the well' must make do with a fleeting mention in my poem.

* a stone with a natural depression or "bowl".

The Well

Where is this well they talk of?
Settled in the ferns
Among hawthorn bushes;
Hidden away from fresh rain,
Waiting a visitor to call again.

And she's waiting to welcome us,
Sleeves dipped in the dappled pool,
Watermark rising,
Hands cupped and whispering a truth.

This guardian of the well and the lost voices
Welcomed me to this festival of healing.
Rags festooned on branches,
Some fresh patterned fabric, neat little edges,
Others, rotting away with the intentions put upon them.

And this pilgrim of the truth
Spoke what I had forgotten,
To kneel upon the moss stone,
To be,
To listen.

Colourful clooties at Madron Holy Well in West Cornwall.

Only the River Roe below, humming and flowing,
Giving shape and movement and life to the town,
Writing and rewriting history as it babbles along.
And those that travel here now are re-routed;
A new and well-deserved peace
Upon this sacred ground.

No one knows us like you do.
No one knows us like you do.

———

Over the years, I've heard of all manner of ways of getting rid of warts, from rubbing bread on the wart and giving it to a donkey to eat, to touching the hem of a coat belonging to a man who's never seen his father without him knowing! I laugh to think that while I was visiting the wart well in Dungiven as a child, Sam was being passed through a hole in a granite standing stone called Mên-an-Tol near his father, Geoffrey's home in West Cornwall, in the hope of preventing rickets (which he didn't get). There's a cure for everything somewhere! I've visited other wells like the one in Dungiven in Cornwall, Wales and Scotland and find that in the midst of our busy modern lives they're wonderful and special places to escape, somewhere in which we can place our trust and be at peace, like our ancestors before us.

OVERLEAF
In the grounds of the old Priory, near the Holy Well.

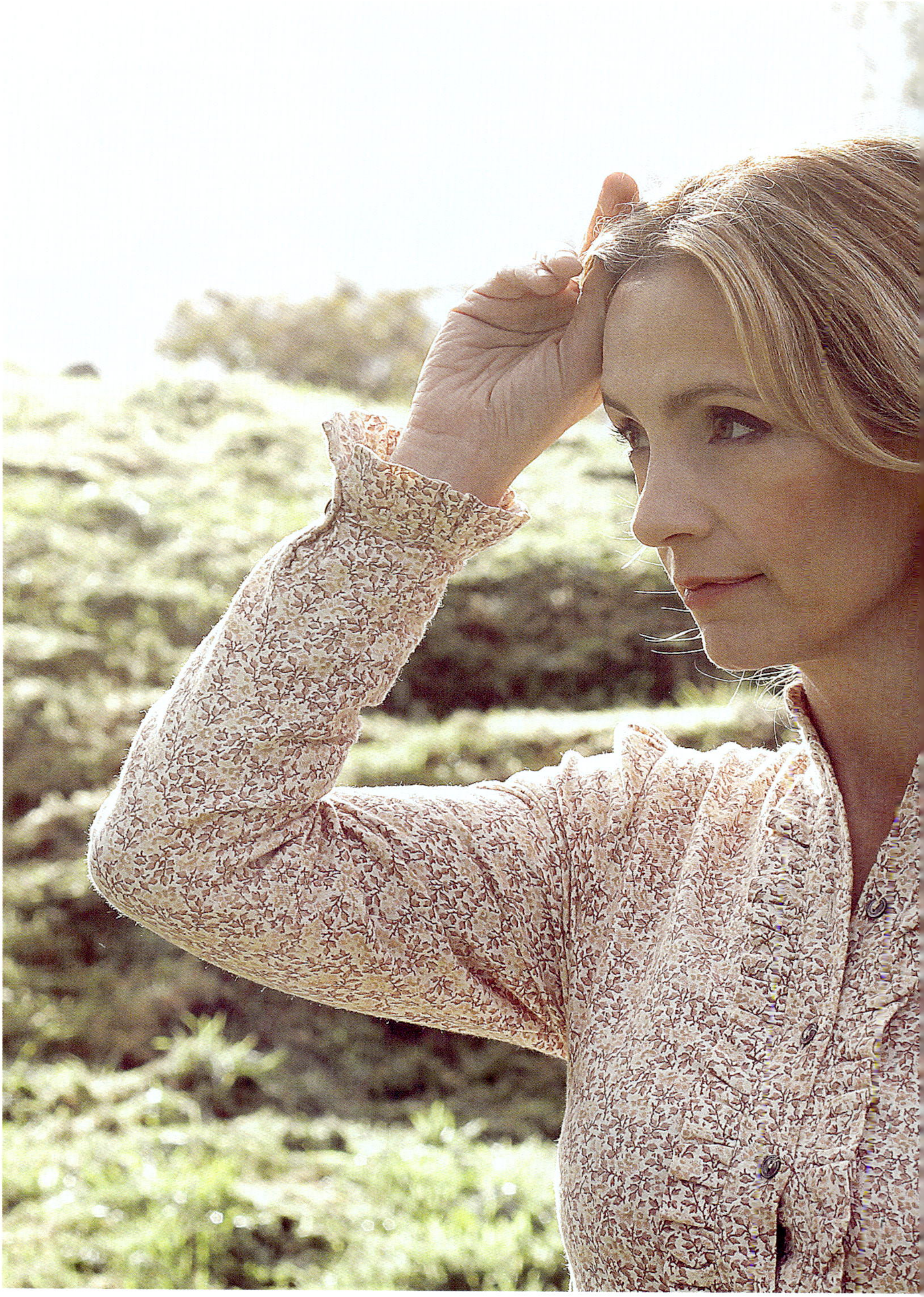

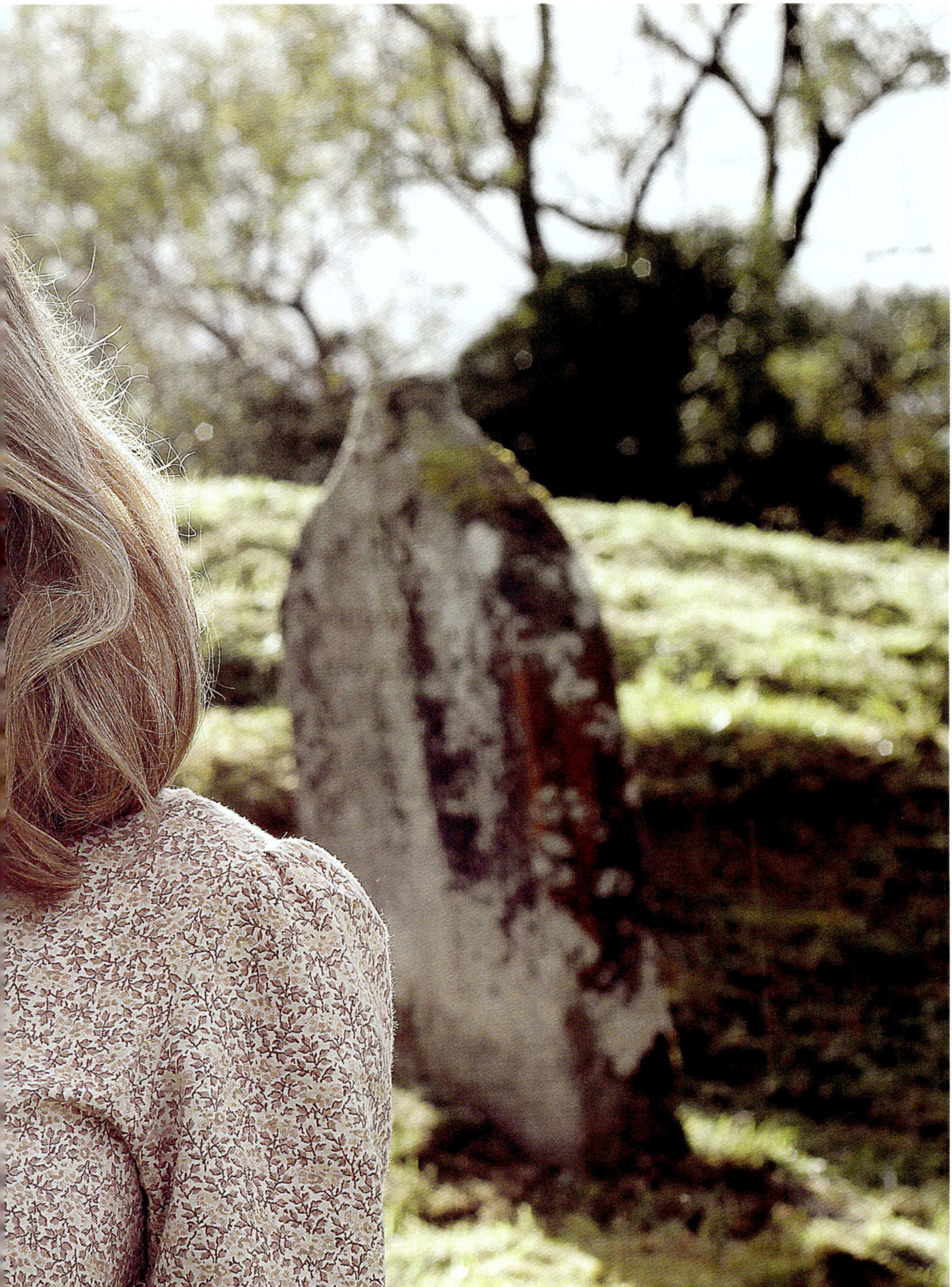

I have my fair share of ailments, some serious, some not too bad. Because I'm a Type 1 diabetic, I have to inject myself multiple times per day, I have hypothyroidism and also suffer from anaemia, so you can imagine that every now and then – when I'm utterly scundered with my fate and feeling burnt out, I go looking for a cure. I don't expect the waters to part and to be healed completely, but I'm looking for something that will nourish my body and soul and help put me back in the right mindset to be the best version of myself.

And so I sent for Carrageen moss, which is not a moss at all but a seaweed which grows off the shores of the Atlantic coast, including Donegal. I remember it being made into milky puddings when I was wee. Being full of vitamins and minerals, it is said to be a great tonic for the body. In fact, the current screensaver picture on my phone is one I took of this beautiful pink Irish seaweed. Anyway, I'm constantly on the lookout for something to help me, like many people who live with a chronic disease. All we want is to be well and to find our own cures.

The old Priory on the outskirts of Dungiven. The Holy Well is just under the trees on the right and the River Roe can be found further down a path beyond the ruins.

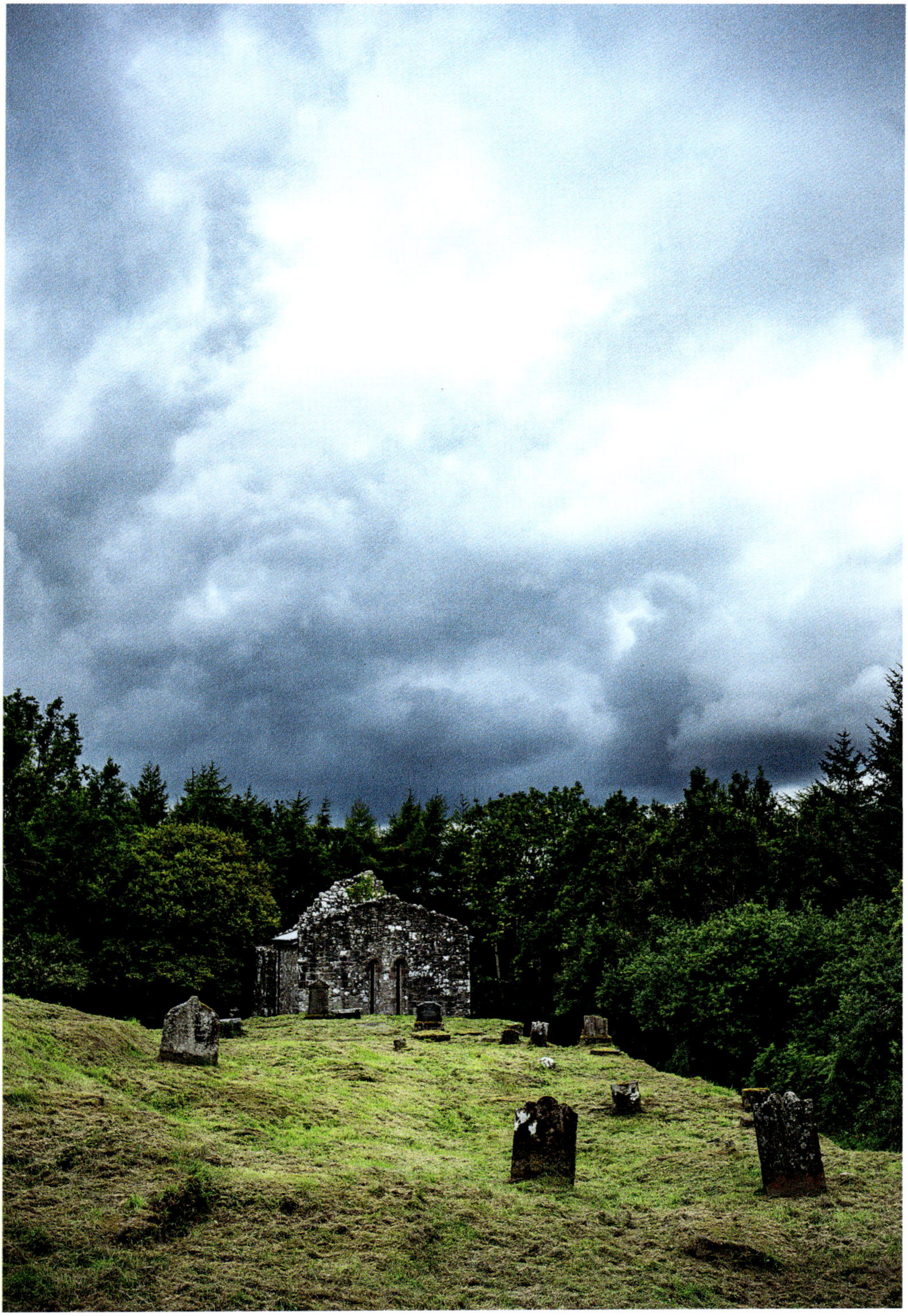

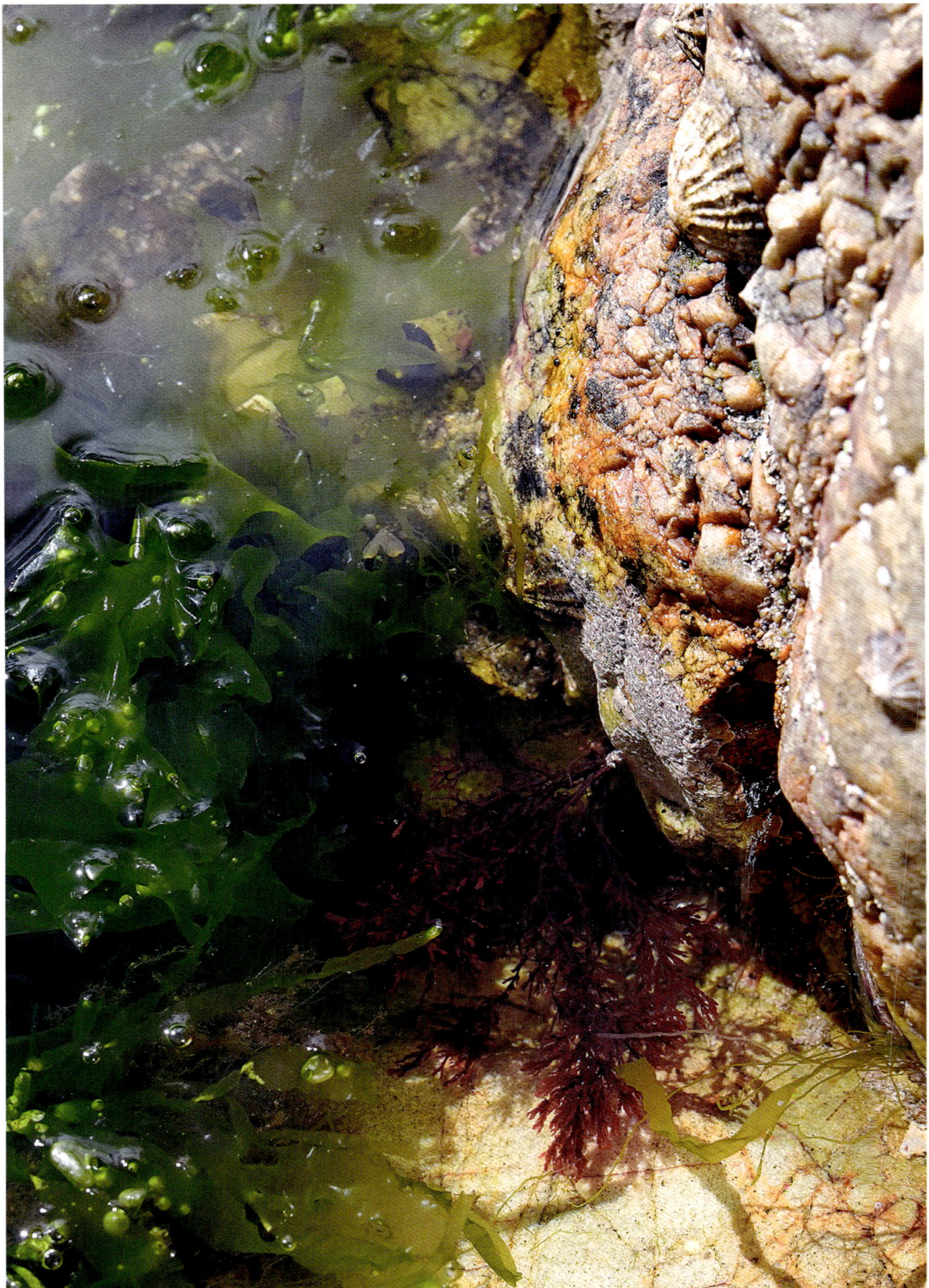

Carrageen Moss

If I could get some Carrageen moss,
I'd wash it and soak it the day's long
And change the water and sing a song.
I'd send for it to Malin
Along the wild Atlantic coast,
For it's there among the pools and inlets,
Chondrus Crispus grows.

I'd treasure this 'Little Rock', as it's known.
And it would nourish and strengthen,
Soothe and clear my soul,
And then my bones.

It's there among the pools and inlets,
Chondrus Crispus grows.
There among the pools and inlets,
Chondrus Crispus grows.

If I could get some Carrageen moss
I'd wash and soak it the day's long.
I'd change the water and sing a song
I'd send to Malin
Along the wild coast.

It's there among the pools and inlets,
Chondrus Crispus grows.
There among the pools and inlets,
Chondrus Crispus grows.

———

Chondrus Crispus.

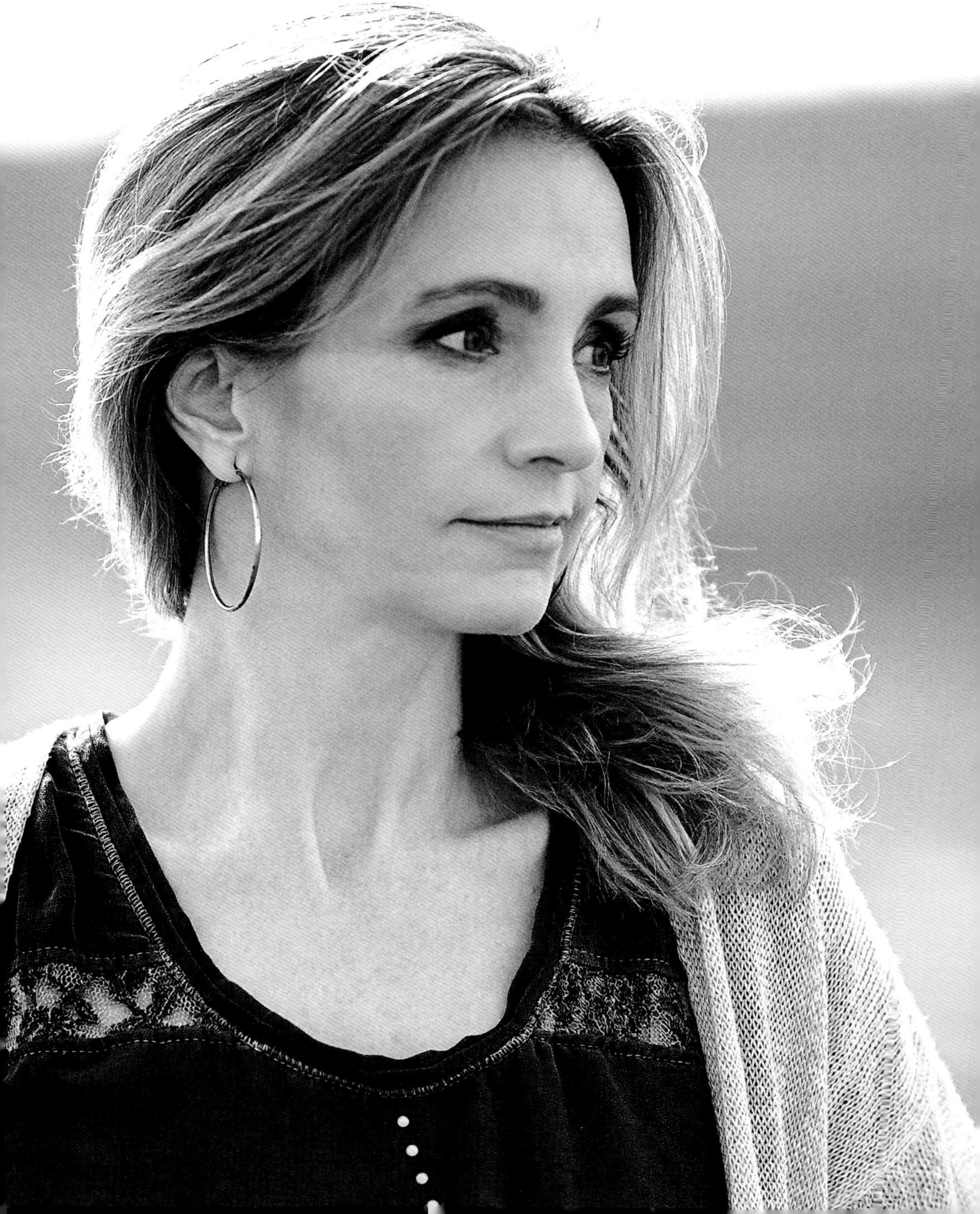

White Sheets

Music has afforded me the privilege to travel all over the world. In this business, the highs are there for all to see – the beautiful lights of a well-lit stage, sold-out concert halls, festivals, winning awards, rapturous applause and the intoxicating loveliness that comes with all of that. There's no doubt these highs can be phenomenal. But I know that I'm luckier than most, for I have my best friend and husband with me at every step of the way. We appreciate these times spent together sharing these amazing experiences, otherwise it all might seem a bit dreamy … and it can be hard (sometimes impossible) to explain to others who weren't there exactly what it's really like. For instance, the day after a scan when we discovered I was carrying twins, Sam and I found ourselves on-stage in a 2,500-year-old Greek amphitheatre in Taormina, Sicily. We were opening for Simple Minds' 10,000-strong audience while also lucky enough to be watching the spectacular sight of Mount Etna throwing red lava into the night sky. It was erupting directly behind the stage. How do you share an experience like that with someone who wasn't there? The truth is, you can't. It was just Sam and I onstage... (Oh, and the babies).

However, it certainly wouldn't be the music business without the lows. I don't plan on listing every grievance and tale of misery here, but I have shared dressing rooms and recording studios with others where I have felt undervalued, I have worked with some who've tried to undermine me, and many times I've felt completely misunderstood. I have sometimes found the music business to be misogynistic, ageist and ignorant and I'm absolutely sure of one thing: if I hadn't had Sam by my side, I'd have packed it all in a long time ago.

As we've both gotten older, we've recognised when to stop and take stock of the various situations we find ourselves in. We've learned it's a great and powerful thing to be able to say "no" ... and believe me, we've said no to a great many things. If we get a strong feeling about a situation, we tend follow our gut. We only ever record music now that moves and inspires us.

The wonderful thing about Sam is that he always gives me the space I need to say what I think. I believe it's how this collection, *Coming Home*, came to be born. He's only ever encouraged me to speak up. In fact, there've been many times he's had to do it for me; and he will never truly know what that has meant to me and how thankful I am – for it is hard to put into words. Perhaps it's clear to him in the moments of music we create together, for they often transcend how we truly express ourselves on this earthly plane.

One thing is crystal-clear though. No matter what I've come through or the trials I've faced, I've felt strength and empowerment whenever I think of the women from my life that I know and love: my mother, aunties, sisters, mother-in-law, and now my friends here in Somerset, strong, hard-working resilient women. I see their lights shining bright in spite of the trials and tribulations they face.

Another thing that has become clearer to me is that I've gotten better at speaking up for myself … although it's frustrating that the more important the situation, the harder it's been to say what I feel. And when the going has gotten really tough, I can always rely on my mammy's voice in my head telling me, "Cara, everything passes and *all* will be well again."

We are lucky that as women we enjoy talking things through with each other. It's easy for us to get together with friends and family and openly share our problems and look for advice. I remember my mother having regular gatherings in the house with her female friends. They'd have drinks and snacks and sort out lots of stuff. She was brilliant, like many women of her generation, at knowing just what was needed, whether it was organising marching women for the civil rights movement or getting meals out to the old folk, helping sort out young mothers who needed baby food and nappies or arranging wakes and weddings. She was the first person to sell used clothing in a corner of her clothing shop in Claudy, before opening a dedicated St Vincent De Paul thrift store in Dungiven, eventually becoming President of St. Vincent De Paul for the area. Often driving to Belfast for meetings, she was always on the go.

"White sheets" flowed very easily from me. I was thinking of the many strong women of Dungiven who've held the town in the palm of their hands, the women who kept us all safe in their hearts and in their prayers, the ones who knew what to do in a crisis, with doors that were open to other women who needed support or advice, the women who stood symbolically side by side, bearing witness to life in the town, enduring all with humility. I use Mammy and the other women I know as my beacons, their (quite-often) formidable reputations going before them.

Mammy often says of her older friends who've passed on, "Isn't it funny? There's not a word about her now she's gone," as if they were a figment of her imagination. So, I suppose this is my ode to them, dead or alive.

Minnie McKenna
Bernie McNicholl
Betty-Ann McNicholl
Teresa Dillon
Ann Brolly
Lucy McCloskey (Vicky)
Bridie Lynch
Anna Mullan
Maura McMacken
Patsy Lowry
Claire McFlynn
Mary K Hinphey
Sinead McNicholl
Margaret Cassidy
Annie Jo Kealey
Mary K Groogan
Madeline Kelly
Katie Coyle

To be honest, this list could go on and on and will only mean something to those who know or knew them. In my mind's eye I see these strong, happy ladies lining the streets of my town, hoping and praying for the next generation, for *their* sons and daughters and grandchildren to lead the way – to then return, brighter, and stronger than ever before.

OVERLEAF
On top of Benbradagh, looking down to Dungiven town.

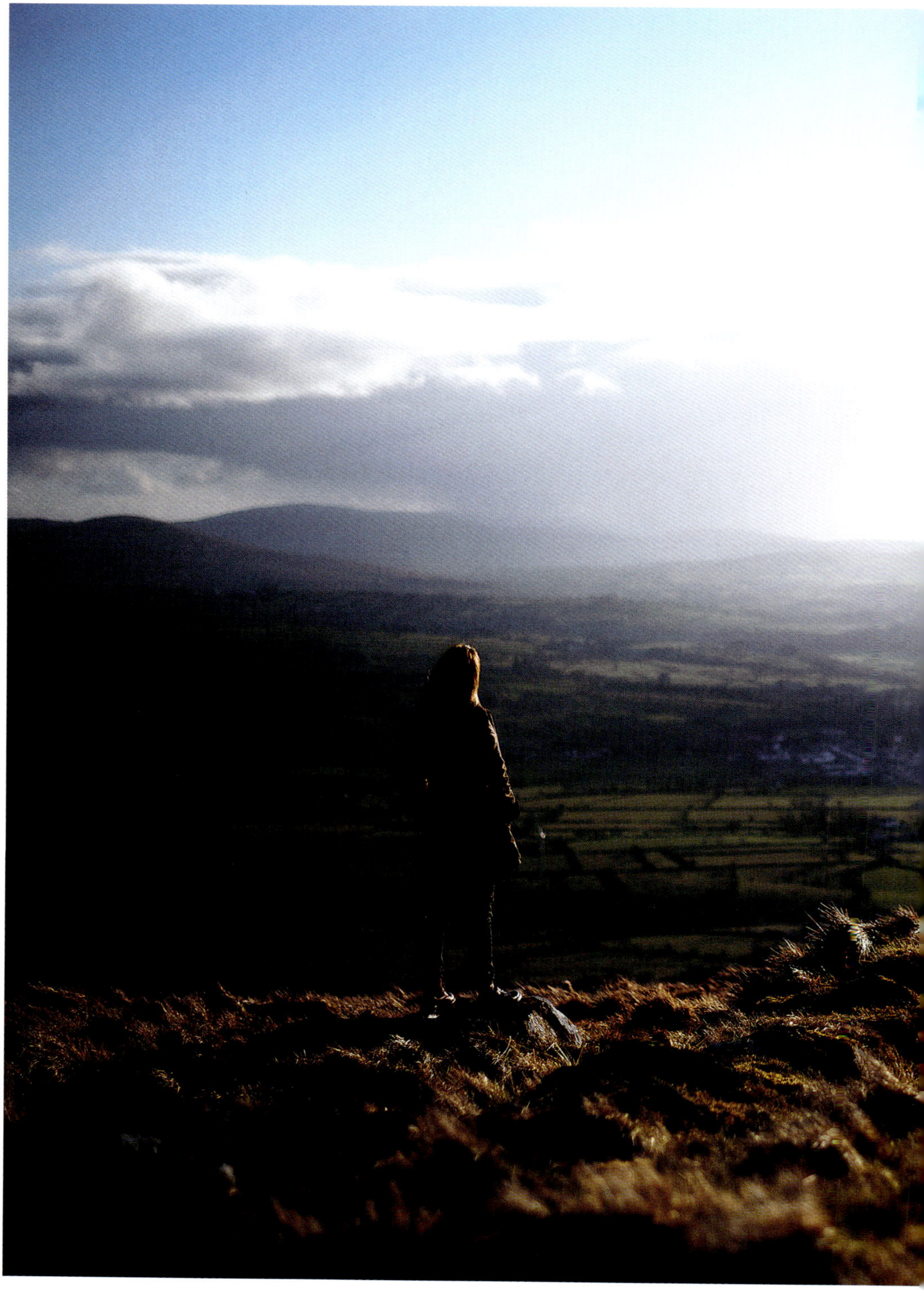

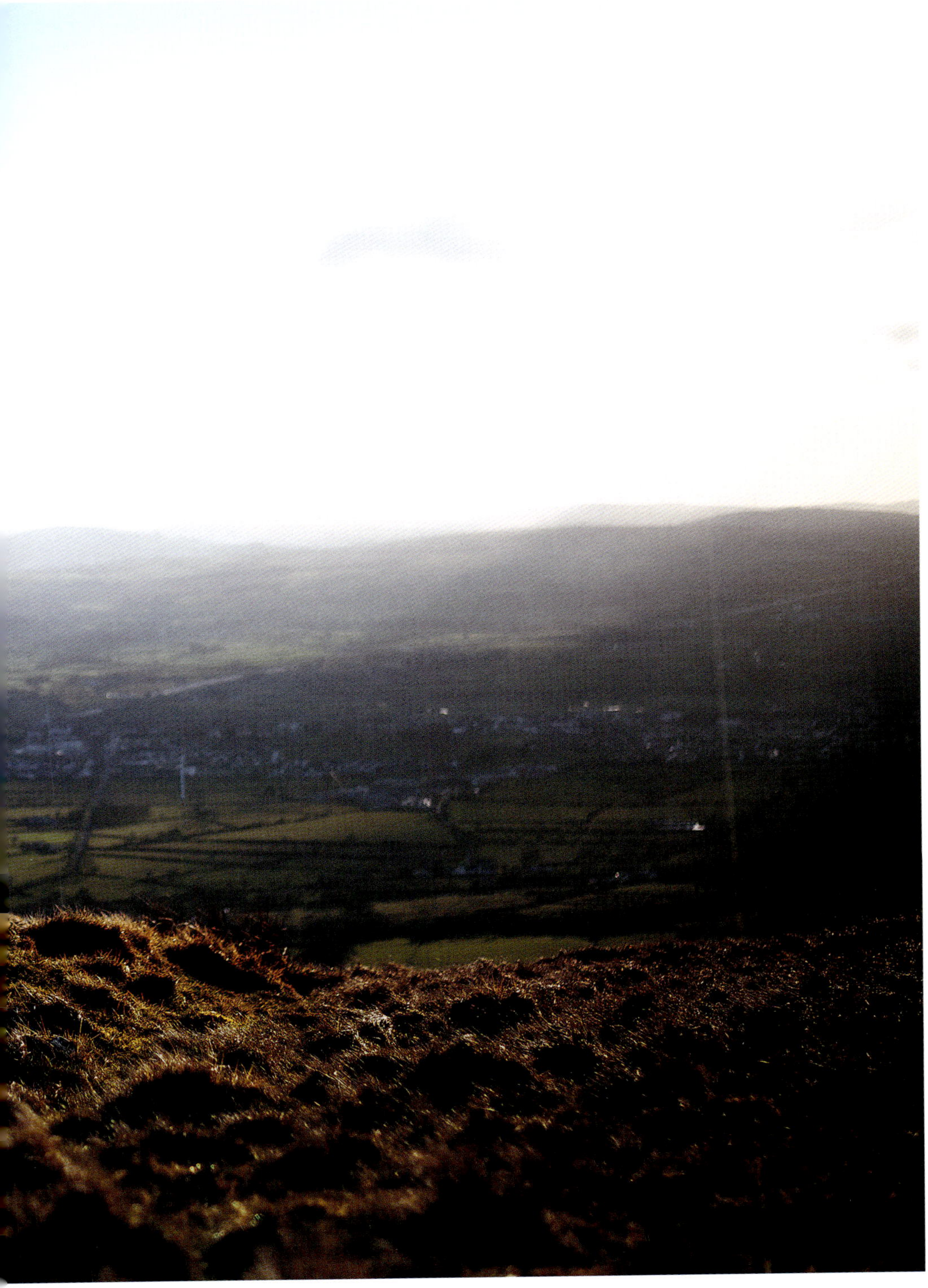

White Sheets

There's not a word about her now she's gone,
Isn't it funny?
And her who held the town in the palm of her hand.
Up and down the main street,
Wasn't it grand to see her, and the step of her?
Sure, you'd know her a mile off.

And she had a wile good turn in her.
She'd give you the last bite in her mouth
If she thought it'd help.
And to see her row of white sheets drying
On a good drying day
Would do your heart good.
To see them skirt and play,
Catching the last breath of autumn
And the ground still dry.

And she was scared to leave,
For fear of being lost.
So her world was here,
Simply uncomplicated.
And she had time,
Time for all of us,
To listen over and over again
Without comment or judgement,
Stepping into the shadows
To let us all find enough light to shine.

And you were safe in her repose.
Her breath guarding and shielding
From the world beyond the latch of her door.
Marmalade and turf infusing the air,
Its smell carried over the Sperrins,
And her …
Going nowhere.

―――

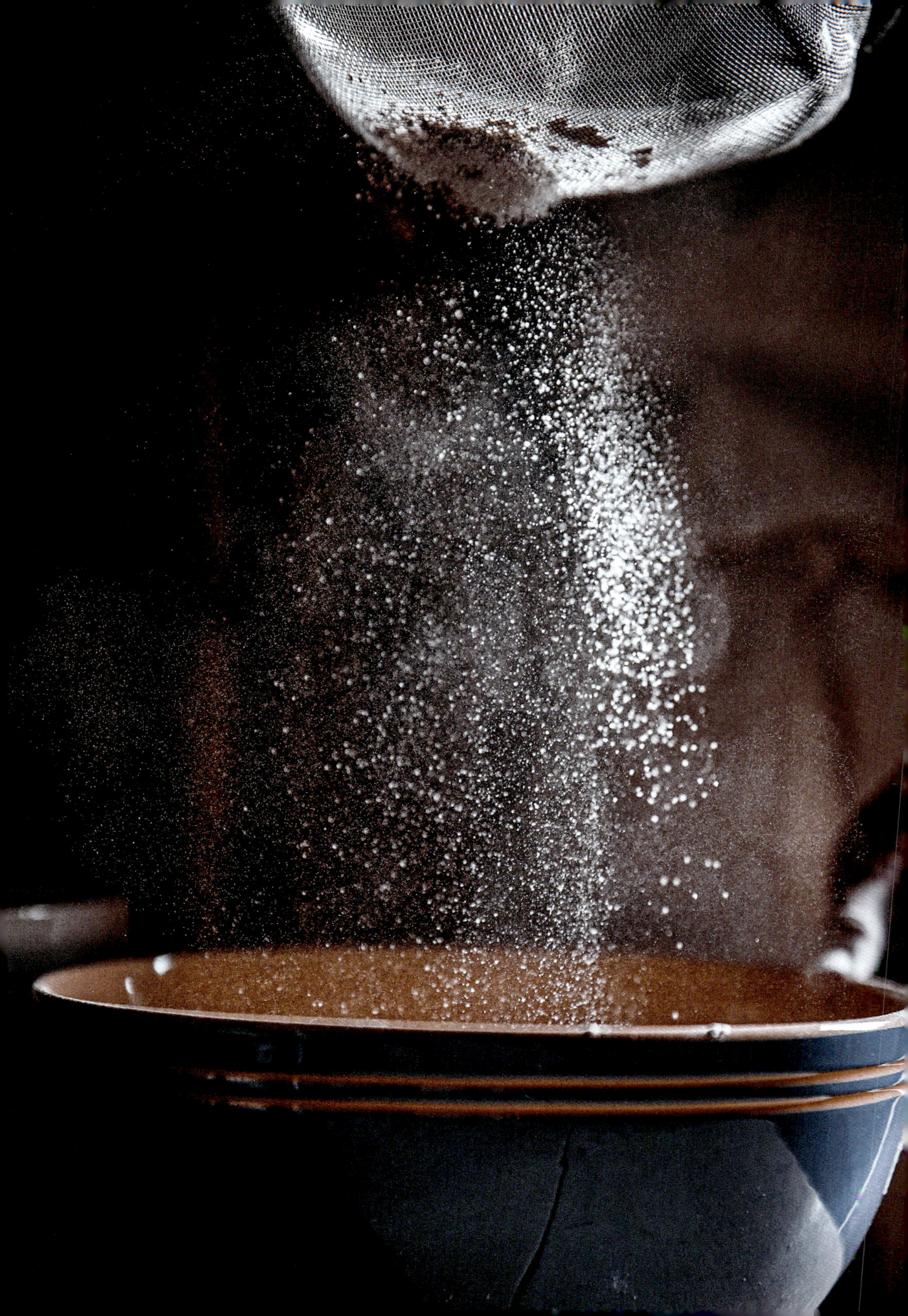

Apron Strings

For those who aren't familiar with traditional soda scones rather than classic afternoon-tea scones, there's not much point in me trying to explain the difference; maybe you could take a moment to look it up. Suffice to say that in my part of the world, soda scones are a pretty big deal. The people who make the best scones always have plenty of friends and happy kitchens.

Some of my happiest memories are when I think back on our kitchen when I was growing up. There was always something cooking and always lots of baking going on to feed the hungry mouths coming in from school and for my father and his workmen who regularly dropped in for a quick cup of tea: buttermilk pancakes, soda bread, wheaten loaves, vegetable soup and an array of delicious cakes that no one seems to make anymore – Black Forest gateau with brandy-soaked cherries and Austrian coffee cakes drowning in rum. These were the best days filled with untidy kitchens, a flour-covered table and very, very, tasty treats.

There always seemed to be dozens of scones piled up on wire racks, accompanied by that amazing smell of scones cooking on the cast-iron griddle on the range. Mammy always had a glass of buttermilk which she would down in one go. She swore blind that this was wile good for you and would line your guts doing you the world of good. I'd always dip my finger into the glass to be sure it tasted as bad as I thought, for she made it look and seem delicious. Then she'd throw her head back and laugh at my sour face of disgust. God only knows how she kept it down.

It was in this kitchen, amid the chaos, where the best *craic* happened. Engagements were announced, weddings were planned and later, babies brought back from the hospital, to this room filled with the smell of comfort and security, the scone dough as soft as each newborn's cheek and their same wee faces sucking and gnawing at them with tea towels tucked round them for bibs. It's the place

A classic Irish saying on my mother's sideboard.

where I was told to rise and give a visitor a seat or "run on now", as neighbours would pull up a chair to confide in my mother over a cup of tea and a scone. I'm pretty sure my mammy made the best scones in the town because there was a steady stream of people through our house to share in them.

I remember once there was a close family friend who wasn't very well at all, and the only thing she could stomach were Teresa Dillon's scones, and so, once a week, a bag was filled for her and taken to her house ... although apparently most were intercepted by her brother and she never even got a lick of one.

Then there was Madeleine Kelly, with whom my mother had a great arrangement. Mammy would bake her famous scones and Madeleine would, in return, provide Mammy with a bag of beautiful knitted slippers which we all benefited from. This arrangement continued for years and years – in fact Sam could barely live without them, so Mammy would

One of my own attempts at soda scones and wheaten bread. I'm still trying to master the art, but they taste pretty good all the same.

often bake batches especially for Sam's slippers!

The act of making scones went back to my mother's own childhood and I'm sure for generations before that. They were cooked over the open fire on a cast-iron griddle in Eslin on the mountainside, feeding a family of eight weans. My mammy talks of her own mother, apparently able to turn her hand to anything, making dresses for all the wee girls in the house out of the old flour bags. She would dye the dresses different colours, and sit with the Tilley lamp by the fireside, singing and sewing night after night – but that's a whole other story…

So what's the key to making these delicious treats? Well, as far as I am aware, it's air … lots and lots of air. Letting the air in, lightly, lightly – easy does it, barely touch them, take your time, stack them and they'll cook away. A written record for my mammy's recipe does not exist, at least not one I know of. I suppose it's all part of the tradition, passing things down from one generation to the next. I make them myself now, though after all these years, I don't feel I get even close to Mammy's level of perfection. I've asked her a few times to tell me her recipe and she says bluntly, "Cara, what way have I reared you? Just add a handful of this and that and you'll know." On asking her once if she did or didn't add an egg, she replied rather ambiguously, "Well if you have one, it wouldn't do any harm to throw it in for a bit of nutrition … if you like."

On one occasion, many years ago, Sam got involved, rolling up his sleeves and watching her like a hawk to see if there was some knack or secret trick that we knew nothing about that made her scones so good. He claims he saw nothing different to how I make them, but the outcome was of course a world apart to my own attempts. I have been told manys the time to "Catch yerself on," and, "What in the name of God is wrong with you, that you can't throw together a handful of flour and buttermilk to make a scone?!" And so my quest for the perfect soda scone continues with my own family and friends eating my efforts.

My aunties also baked scones, so understandably there was more than a little competition going on, not to mention scrutiny: "Jaysus, they're raw in the middle! You couldn't eat 'em ... they'd give you wile heartburn!" This was never said to their faces of course.

Then there is the question of whether they should or shouldn't be cut into triangles. I know it may seem trivial but it made for some good gossip!

But regardless of who made them, the effect was almost always the same: putting butter on warm scones was pure heaven! Then the next day frying them in the bacon fat on the pan was almost as good as – and in some cases better than – the day before.

It must be because I live away from home that this ritual has become so important to me – a core memory. I now view it as an important part of my own culture and I celebrate and almost covet the act. In fact, this Mother's Day, I treated myself to a bottle of Mammy's perfume and made some griddle scones so that I could be close in a way to my mother – to be transported right back to those moments again. Thankfully they were gobbled up by my own family – my constant criticising of them falling on hungry teenagers' deaf ears.

OVERLEAF
Me and Mammy making soda scones in her kitchen...well, Mammy making scones, and me watching to see where I'm going wrong.

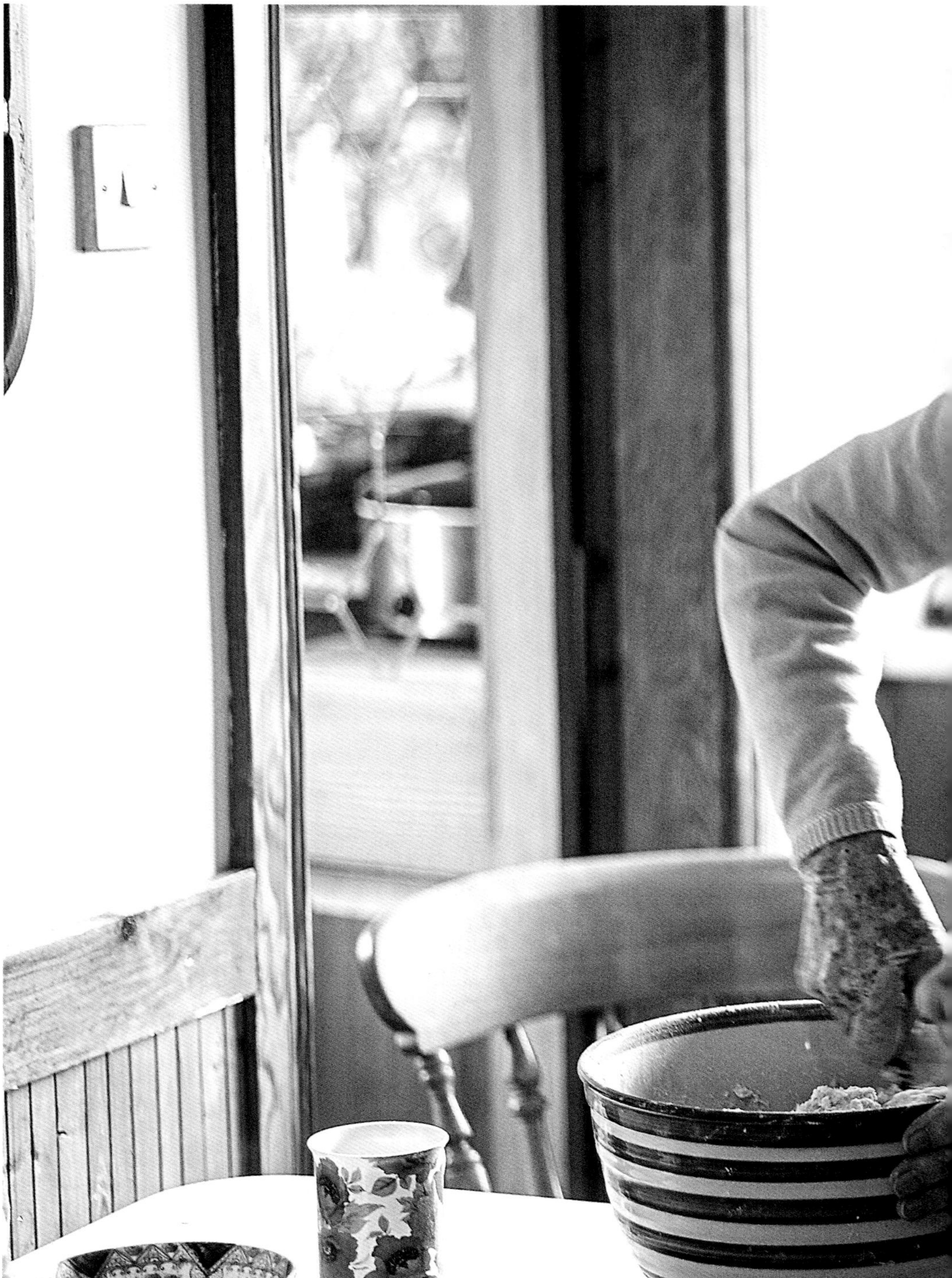

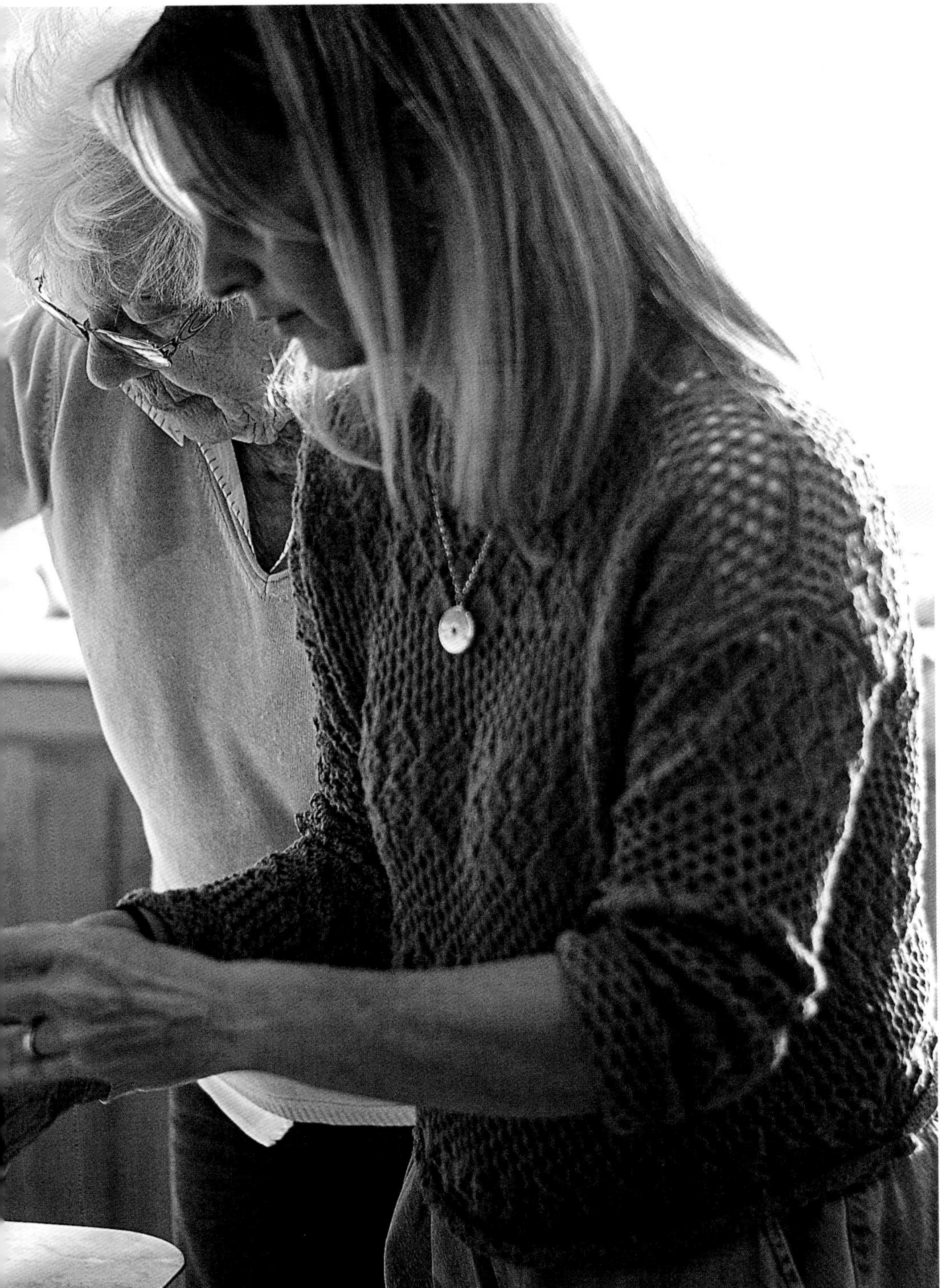

Apron Strings

I liked the way you tied the bow on your apron.
These little things, and you'd never know I watched
The flour, and the colour of your hands,
And the dough, not even as soft as the palm of your hand.

Rings off and rings on,
Heating up to bake your scones.
A half dozen now,
A half dozen more,
And some for us, and then some more.
A wheen for her, a couple for them, and them.

Round and round,
Dough stretching and pulling
Against the metal spoon,
Turning and airing.
It'll be time enough soon.
Time when the flour dust fills the air
And falls upon us in layers,
Settling on every surface,
Settling and waiting, like us, for the stories.

And they come, soon enough,
Spilling off your tongue,
As easy as the eggs you crack, one by one.
Your mixture is slapped 'til it comes to life,
And there's laughter and there's sour buttermilk.
You drink a glass, it's what you do,
It's your culture, it's your art.

Now gently tuck in your rounds,
Lightly does it. Wait, stop! You'll ruin it.
And here too, in this moment, there's a fine line,
A delicate balance for the life that's in it.
We watch them rise, we wait our turn,
We stack them side by side in cosy lines,
Tea towels tucked round them like baby clothes,
Just as I now do with mine.

OVERLEAF
In front of Eslin.

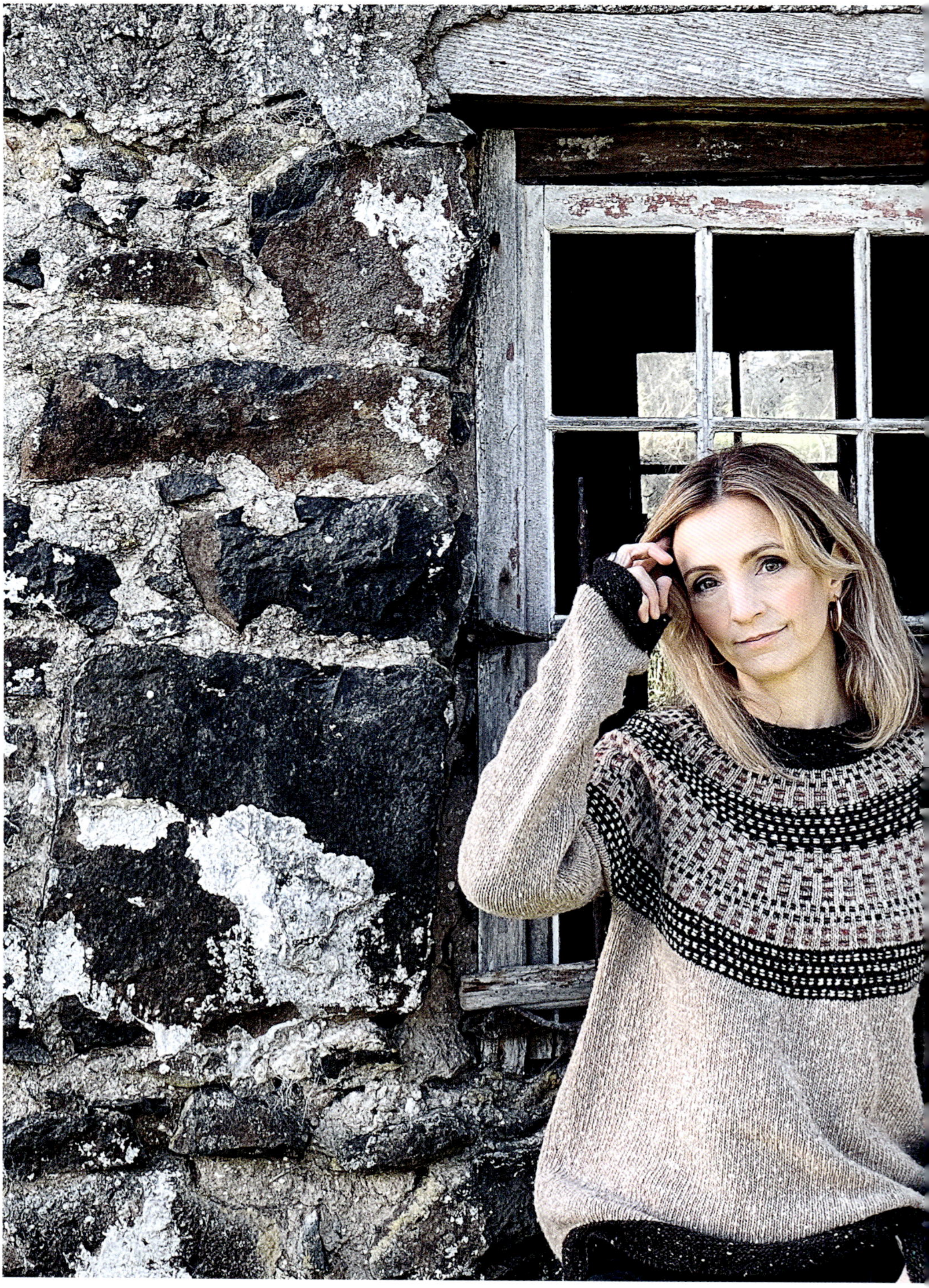

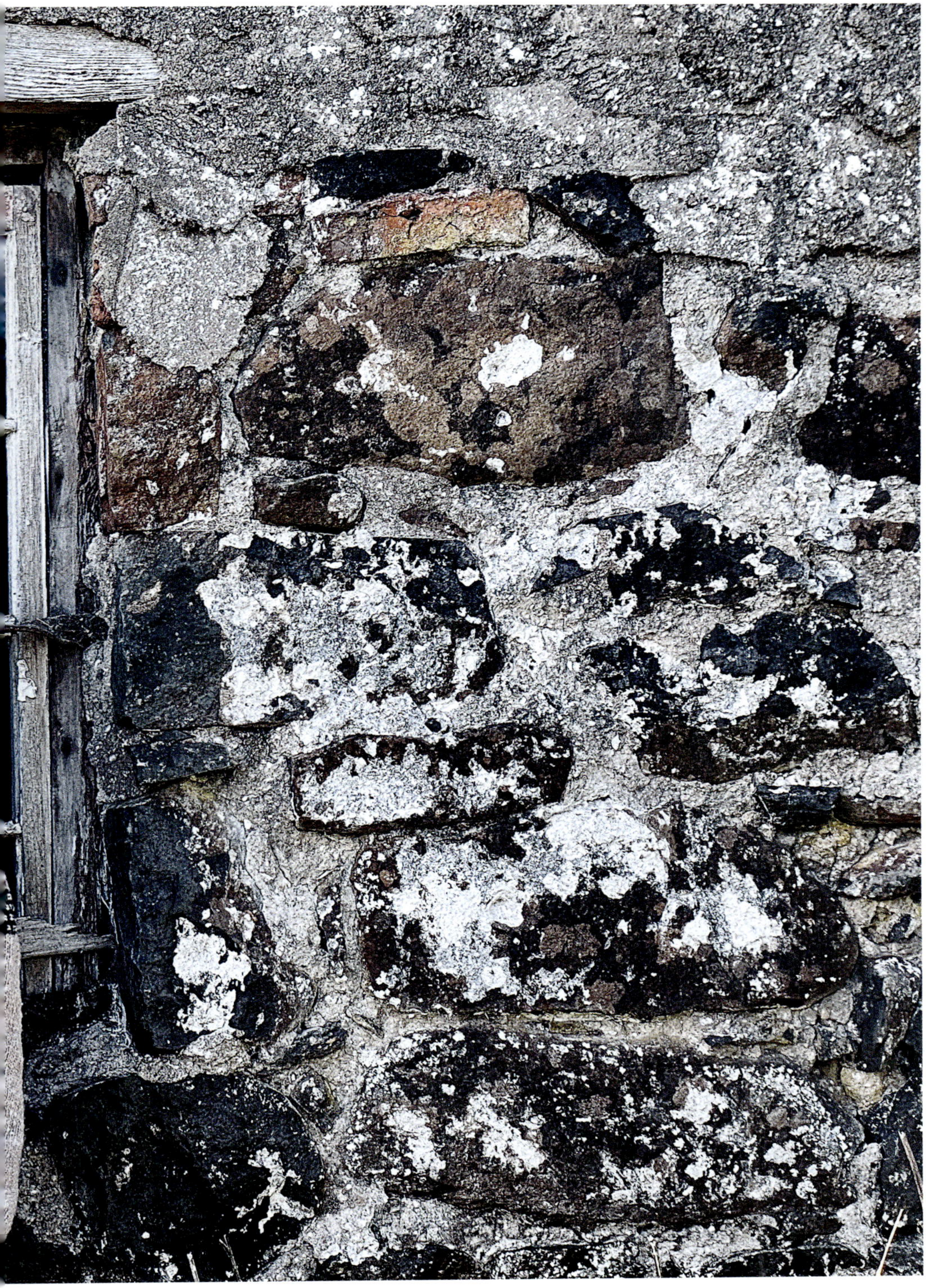

Acknowledgments

To my husband, Sam. Only a few of us are lucky enough to have someone to share our dreams with and watch them become reality. You are my North Star, forever guiding me to where I need to be. You were absolutely crucial in the making of this book. Everything I do, I do for us and you have my heart forever.

To my mother. Thank you for your patience, wisdom and understanding. The memories we share will forever keep me company.

To my children. Thank you for putting up with my emotional ramblings, and with me filling the kitchen table with my messy notes.

To my sisters and brother: branches of the tree. We stand strong together, rooted deep by the love shown to us by our parents. We are all different versions of each other and I love you all.

To Odhrán. Thank you for telling me to "get on with it", for your endless support and creative contribution, I'm blessed to have you so close to my home and my heart.

To Joy and Geoff. I am forever grateful to you for listening, your encouragement gave me faith and confidence.

Me and Sam.

Biography

Few are as revered as Cara Dillon. She has earned her place as one of the most celebrated singers in Ireland. Her breadth of appeal stems from a remarkable career that continually places her home and culture at the very heart of her music and began with her singing with legendary Irish bands like De Dannan as a teenager, being signed to iconic indie record label Rough Trade, touring throughout the world, contributing the title track and narration for a Disney movie and collaborating with Symphony Orchestras in Ireland, England, Scotland and beyond. Having formed a long and successful musical partnership with her husband, Sam Lakeman, they have steered an eclectic path. In doing so she has garnered consistent acclaim from adoring fans, critics and fellow artists alike. Steeped in the culture of her native Co. Derry, she continues to sing with a passion and confidence earned through a lifetime's experience singing traditional songs.

Album Catalogue

Cara Dillon, (2001) Rough Trade

Sweet Liberty, (2003) Rough Trade

After the Morning, (2006) Rough Trade

Hill of Thieves, (2009) Charcoal Records

A Thousand Hearts, (2014) Charcoal Records / Sony

Upon a Winter's Night (2016) Charcoal Records

Wanderer, (2017) Charcoal Records

Live At Cooper Hall, (2021) Charcoal Records

Coming Home, (2024) Charcoal Records

Only Cara's solo releases are included in this list.

To order books, collector's editions, signed LPs or CDs, handwritten lyrics and other merchandise please go to:

www.caradillon.co.uk

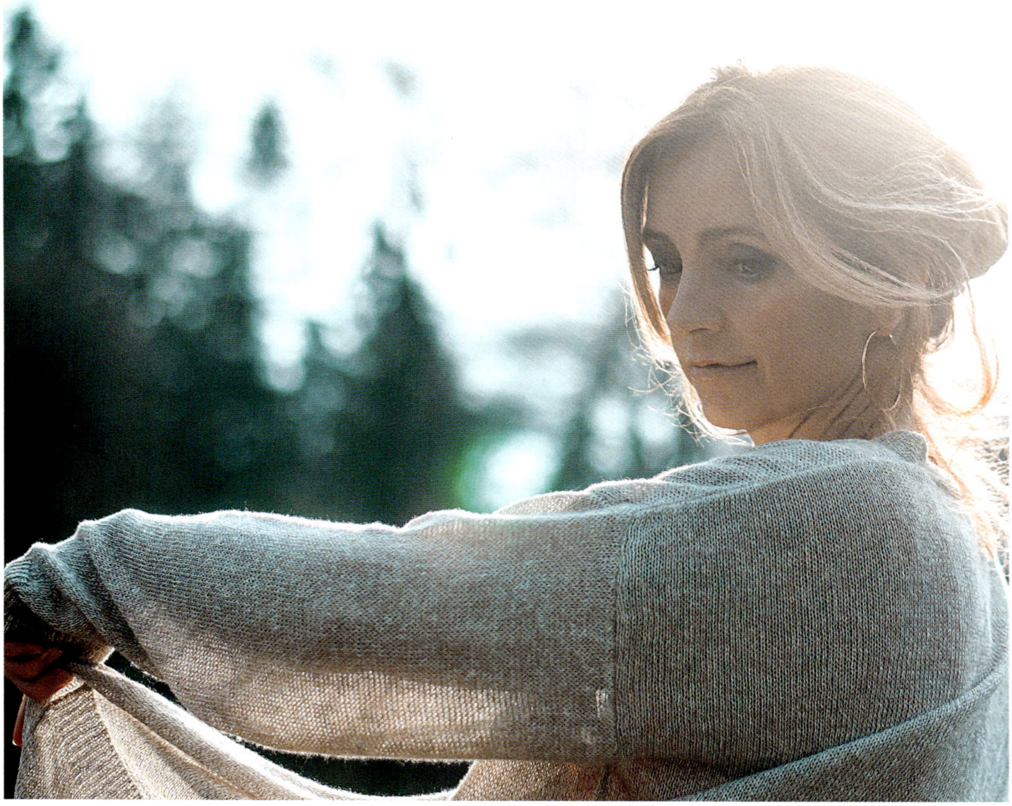